ZOMBIES, FOOTBALL AND THE GOSPEL

ENDORSEMENTS

"Innovation requires honest assessment of where we are and where we're going. By keeping an eye on what's happening around us, Reggie Joiner points the way going forward in the midst of extraordinary change."

MARK BATTERSON
LEAD PASTOR, NATIONAL COMMUNITY CHURCH & AUTHOR, *CIRCLE MAKER*

"Zombies, Football, and the Gospel opens up an authentic conversation about why the church our kids will inherit won't be like the church where we grew up. The realities described in this book are more than trends ... they're the new normal. Reggie has really made me think with this one!"

DOUG FIELDS
YOUTH MINISTRY VETERAN & AUTHOR, *PURPOSE DRIVEN MINISTRY*

"Reggie Joiner shows us what it means to be a game-changer. His insights on the church and how we can more effectively be the church in this ever-changing culture always challenge and inspire me. This book will do the same for you."

JEFF HENDERSON
LEAD PASTOR, GWINNETT CHURCH

"Once again, Reggie Joiner challenges us to rethink our ministries in Zombies, Football and the Gospel. This book encourages you to consider what's transformed you, your life and your world and then forces you to think even further."

SHERRY SURRATT
CEO & PRESIDENT, MOTHERS OF PRESCHOOLERS INTERNANTIONAL

"Reggie passionately paints a picture of what is at stake for every church committed to reaching the next generation. He inspires us to wrestle through the tough issues finding the best way to showcase what really works. After reading Zombies, Football and the Gospel, my passion to see the local church prevail while facing unprecedented challenges is white hot!"

SUE MILLER
LEADERSHIP DEVELOPMENT, ORANGE & AUTHOR, *MAKING YOUR CHILDREN'S MINISTRY THE BEST HOUR OF EVERY KID'S WEEK*

COPYRIGHT

Zombies, Football and the Gospel
Published by Orange, a division of The reThink Group, Inc.
5870 Charlotte Lane, Suite 300
Cumming, GA 30040 U.S.A.

The Orange logo is a registered trademark of The reThink Group, Inc.

All Scripture quotations, unless otherwise noted, are taken from the Holy Bible, New International Version®. NIV®. Copyright © 1973, 1978, 1984 by International Bible Society. Used by permission of Zondervan.

Other Orange products are available online and direct from the publisher. Visit our website at www.WhatIsOrange.org for more resources like these.

ISBN: 978-0-9854116-1-9

©2012 Reggie Joiner
©2012 The reThink Group, Inc.

Writers: Reggie Joiner
The reThink Group Editing Team: Jennifer Davis, Elizabeth Hansen, Kristen Ivy, Mike Jeffries, Melanie Williams, Karen Wilson
Design: Ryan Boon & FiveStone

Printed in the United States of America
First Edition 2012

1 2 3 4 5 6 7 8 9 10

04/16/12

ZOMBIES, FOOTBALL AND THE GOSPEL

THE ART OF COLLABORATION

I have been living in the context of team for the past few decades. So I don't even know how to think, write, produce, dream, or do anything without collaboration. I am extremely grateful for the people who play on our team. Their passion for the mission of the church is contagious. Some contributors are listed in the back of the book.

Those who spent time doing editorial, and design were an integral part of this project. Their fingerprints are all over these pages. They include ... Jen Davis, Kristen Ivy, Mike Jeffries, Tim Walker, Melanie Williams, Karen Wilson. And our art design team included Ryan Boon & FiveStone.

Together we have learned that you
...Improv or Die.

TABLE OF CONTENTS

INTRODUCTION

THERE ARE MOMENTS
IN YOUR LIFE WHEN

EVERYTHING CHANGES

because of a
REVELATION

because of an
EXPERIENCE

because of a
RELATIONSHIP

RESHAPE
who you are

THESE
MOMENTS
CAN CAUSE
YOU TO

REDEFINE
how you live

RETHINK
what you do

They have happened in the past.

A German mathematician theorized that the earth revolved around the sun.
Crowds of angry American colonists dumped tea into the Boston Harbor.
Scientists split an atom to create the ultimate weapon.
An African-American refused to give up her seat on an Alabama bus.
A Mississippi musician mixed rhythm and blues with country.
Chinese college students gathered to protest in Tiananmen Square.
Harvard students created a website to help everyone on campus connect socially.

It is interesting how—
- a significant event in time can become a catalyst to change the future
- a revolutionary idea can influence the mindset of an entire generation
- a cultural shift can make a radical impact in social norms

THESE ARE
GAME-CHANGERS.

A game-changer is something that requires you to radically alter the way you play.

That is, if you want to win.

GAME-CHANGERS
CAN TRANSFORM YOUR PERSONAL LIFE.

Or your professional life. This book focuses on the way game-changers can revolutionize your ministry.

If you learn to identify game-changers when they occur, you can make the adjustment you need to be an effective leader.

If you ignore them, you could become stagnant and irrelevant.

I am fortunate that I get to hang out with people smarter than I am, and collectively discover ideas and innovations that change how we work and live.

So, here's my list of game-changers. I'm not suggesting this is the only list. I don't even think it's the best list. It's just my list.

How did I come up with it? Well, it was actually a very scientific process.

This list is a result of an in-depth survey with over 2,000 Christian leaders from 30 different denominations who live in diverse regions of the country.

Actually, that's not true. I asked a dozen leaders who trust what they thought. Then I wrote down a list of things I wanted to say.

So, keep these things in mind:

THIS LIST IS NOT COMPLETE
I'm not sure it's possible to have a complete list of things that need to change if they are going to keep changing.

THIS LIST IS NOT THEOLOGICAL
This is not a Bible study. I'm assuming you already do that. This is a challenge to at least understand culture before you attempt to influence it. It's what missionaries do.

THIS LIST IS NOT SCIENTIFIC
I'm not qualified to do official research. But these ideas do reflect various data, and insights from key leaders around the country I chose to focus mostly on what seem to be the cultural shifts when you compare this information. But trust me, I will keep asking experts where I'm right and wrong and let you know what I find out.

For now, this is what I think. And all I'm asking you to do is to think about it too.

Isn't that what most writers do? Write what they think they know, so others can take a shot at correcting it.

Oh, and one more thing. I look forward to discussing these issues more in the future. But I really don't want to get into any ugly, knock-down, drag-out debates about things that typically become the subject of endless blog chains that over-analyze issues we probably won't figure out until we get to heaven.

Frankly, I don't have that kind of time. My life is well over the halfway mark. So, I'm trying to spend the days I have left: helping incredible leaders and churches continue to win in their mission, hanging out with anyone who wants to know more about God, eating good food with friends and family, and riding motorcycles.

I hope you will make a note of the game-changers on this list that resonate with you and add some of your own.

We need more opportunities for leaders to collaborate. You can post them at RestlessLeaders.com.

HERE WE GO.

THE GOSPEL IS MESSY

NEVER SETTLE FOR A VERSION OF FAITH THAT DOESN'T TAKE RISKS

1

That's what the Gospel does.

So, how does the Gospel fit into a book designed to get leaders thinking about current game-changers?

Is there something new about the Gospel we don't know?

No.

But this generation has some new ideas about what the Gospel should move us to do.
It places renewed value on the mission of the Gospel.

When Jesus stepped onto the planet, things got messy.

He messed with the ...

traditional practices **of those who were religious.**
customary labels **that defined who was good and bad.**
cultural prejudices **toward distinct people groups.**
political structure **of an evil empire.**

This generation believes the Gospel is not messy enough. Today, people want to trade in their carpeted, air-conditioned, Sunday school version of the Gospel for something that compels them to make a risky collision with a hurting world.

JESUS HAD A WAY OF CHANGING THE RULES.

WHEN THE PHARISEES BROUGHT UP THE LAW	WHEN THE PHARISEES QUOTED SCRIPTURE	WHEN THE PHARISEES ACCUSED SINNERS
JESUS TALKED ABOUT LOVE.	JESUS ADDED SOME NEW IDEAS.	JESUS FORGAVE THEM.

This makes conventional leadership nervous. That's why it's a game-changer. Some leaders are worried that a generation is going to abandon the true meaning of the Gospel for a version that is too social.

BUT WHAT IF THIS IS A REVIVAL THE CHURCH DESPERATELY NEEDS?

We need to be careful we don't water down the passion of this generation.

Of course it's risky. But all the indicators suggest that this generation is tired of an insular, overprotective version of church. There is a resurgence of thought that suggests **the Gospel is messy,** and it calls us to get messy.

THERE'S A GROWING FRUSTRATION WITH CHURCHES WHO DO NOT RESPOND PASSIONATELY TO A BROKEN WORLD.

Geoffrey Canada grew up in Harlem. He attended Mount Pleasant Grove Baptist Church, 137th Street. His grandfather was the pastor. As a teenager, Geoffrey claimed he couldn't reconcile what was happening inside the church with what was happening outside the church. This is the question that bothered him about his grandfather's church. "How can they be spending so much time saving the saved, when the people who needed saving are on the streets every Sunday, and not in the church? So Geoffrey dropped out of the church. He went to Harvard and then moved back to Harlem. He started the Harlem Children's Zone in 1990 to reform education in the neighborhoods where he grew up.

"Most Millennial Christians see local churches as business as usual, focused inwardly, more concerned about the needs of the members than the needs of the community and nations."[1] The U.S. Government's Office for Nonprofits is being overwhelmed with applications, and most of those applications are coming from Millennials. According to the author of *True Religion*, "Their aim is not to grow massive aid or charity organizations. They are far more organic than that. They are simply living their passions. They are responding to the needs of desperate people that grip their heart."[2] That's why this generation is responsible for an upturn in volunteering. According to the Nonprofit Report, "Led by teens and young adults accounting for almost half the increase, about a million more people volunteered last year."[3]

In You Lost Me, David Kinnaman says that apparently this generation is "prepared to be not merely hearers of doctrine but doers of faith; they want to put their faith in action, not just to talk."[4]

A generation is not walking away from the church because they haven't heard the story of the Gospel. They're exiting because they were never invited into the mission of the Gospel. I recently had a conversation with a 22-year-old who left the church when she was 15. She explained, "They taught me what they wanted me to know about all of the stories when I was a kid, but I was never really invited to be a part of the discussion or to do anything significant. I feel like the church is a super-exclusive club that I'm too poor and female to get into."

Am I suggesting it's not important to make sure kids understand the story of the Gospel? Of course not. The story of the Gospel should drive everything we teach. But here's something I also know. I've interviewed hundreds of college students who left the church. I haven't met one yet who told me they abandoned the idea of Christianity because their church never fully explained the story of the Gospel.

I do believe this generation definitely craves a deeper understanding of the narrative of

A GENERATION IS NOT WALKING AWAY FROM THE CHURCH BECAUSE THEY HAVEN'T HEARD THE STORY OF THE GOSPEL. THEY'RE EXITING BECAUSE THEY WERE NEVER INVITED INTO THE MISSION OF THE GOSPEL.

Scripture. But connecting their personal lives to that story in a relevant way is something you must do if you want to re-engage them.

Not that the evangelical old guard hasn't cared, or hasn't served others, but we are seeing a seismic shift in emphasis—from an emphasis on assenting to the right theological ideas and getting to heaven, to one where it's all about translating belief into righteous action on behalf of others. You can expect to find, on a scale not seen for decades, more and more Bible-believing Christians on the front lines of compassion campaigns for the poor, abused women, modern-day slaves, children (born as well as unborn), minorities of every sort, and anyone else being exploited and mistreated,[5] (*USA Today*).

This past January, I watched 40,000 college students at the Passion Conference light a candle and gather to declare war against human and sex trafficking. They gave $2.6 million dollars over three days.

THEY WERE COMPELLED BY A GOSPEL THAT IS MESSY.

Almost every credible researcher, from Baylor to Fuller, from Barna to *USA Today*, is suggesting the same thing: **This generation has become impatient with our theological spin and labels**. They want to engage in something that takes them beyond the endless blog debates.

It's as if they are saying ...

"It is the mission, stupid.
While you talk about it,
we're going to jump into a
messy world.
Yes, we'll make sure people know
the Gospel.
Yes, we'll do it in the name of Jesus."

"But could we please stop arguing,
and just do it?"

This generation doesn't need a new and improved version of Sunday school.
They need to engage in a passionate adventure outside the walls of a church building.

THIS GENERATION DOESN'T NEED A NEW AND IMPROVED VERSION OF SUNDAY SCHOOL. THEY NEED TO ENGAGE IN A PASSIONATE ADVENTURE OUTSIDE THE WALLS OF A CHURCH BUILDING.

A national study by the Search Institute found that "young people who are involved in service are much more likely to be firmly bonded to their churches, much less likely to drop out of school, less likely to engage in behaviors that put them at risk," and have a higher intrinsic motivation toward a future career.[6]

The Gospel is messy.
I have spent almost half a century listening to leaders discuss the Gospel. I've concluded that Mark Driscoll, John Piper, T.D. Jakes, Joel Osteen, and Rob Bell at least agree about one thing.

 Jesus was God's son.
Lived a sinless life.
Died on a cross for my sin.
And came back to life.

The simple Gospel story should put us all on the same page.
Beyond that description, theology can get confusing and complicated. But I'll try to sum up what I'm trying to say another way ... ↓

Jesus didn't live to set a good example.	Jesus didn't die so I could be happy.	Jesus didn't come back to life to prove He was God.	Jesus didn't leave me here so I would get excited about heaven.
↓	↓	↓	↓
He lived sinless so He could die for us.	**He died so I could be forgiven.**	**He came back to life to destroy sin and death.**	**He left me here to take His Gospel to a messy world.**

I think if you interviewed the first-century believers, you would see the Gospel is messy. Following Jesus was complicated, hard and costly. The story of the typical disciple was not characterized by prosperity and a happily-ever-after tale. They did, however, experience a life fully engaged in a mission that compelled them to invite their world into a bigger story of restoration and redemption.

Whenever we promote a version of the Gospel that doesn't take risks, we nurture ...

... a faith that's shallow.
... a faith that's never stretched.
... a faith that never learns to depend on what only God can do.

 SO, GET READY TO TAKE SOME RISKS.

A MESSY GOSPEL COULD COMPEL YOUR CHURCH TO...

LOVE those who don't share your beliefs and values

CREATE new ways to share your message

BECOME MISSIONARIES to diverse cultures

SHOW COMPASSION to broken and hurting people

RE-IMAGINE how you live as the church

CHANGE how you influence the next generation

COLLABORATE with leaders who are different

That's why we are starting here. The Gospel sets the stage for us to reconsider a host of things that face today's church.

As leaders we are called to strategically and consistently rethink what we do for the sake of our mission.

We are responsible to guard whatever is timeless, then be open to changing anything else ...

for the sake of the Gospel.

At least that's how Paul explained his missionary strategy to reach a diverse culture:

I have become all things to all people so that by all possible means I might save some. I do all this for the sake of the Gospel.[7]

This generation just seems ready to embrace a version of faith that is willing to care and love the people around them, regardless of the risks.

MAYBE THE CHURCH SHOULD TAKE A CUE AND FOLLOW THEIR EXAMPLE.

THIS GENERATION JUST SEEMS READY TO EMBRACE A VERSION OF FAITH THAT IS WILLING TO CARE AND LOVE THE PEOPLE AROUND THEM, REGARDLESS OF THE RISKS.

IT'S YOUR TURN: COLLABORATE

WHAT IS ONE THING YOU CAN CHANGE IN YOUR LIFE OR
YOUR MINISTRY FOR THE SAKE OF THE GOSPEL—EVEN IF
IT GETS MESSY?

Take time for me - refuel
daily - not worrying what
does or doesn't get done.

HERE ARE SOME IDEAS
ADD YOUR OWN

1   **2**   **3**

PERSONALIZE IT
FOR YOU

STRATEGIZE IT
WITH YOUR TEAM

ORANGIFY IT
FOR THE NEXT
GENERATION

Carve out time in your personal calendar to participate in a mission trip, or get involved in an effort that targets local social issues.

Discover the core social problems that are happening in your community. Look for ways to establish meaningful partnerships to serve key organizations.

Reorganize your ministries so kids and students have more opportunities to serve in and outside your church.

NEVER SETTLE FOR A VERSION OF FAITH THAT DOESN'T TAKE RISKS

WELCOME TO 98118

LEARN TO BE A GOOD NEIGHBOR IN A COMPLEX CULTURE

2

HERE'S WHAT I KNOW
ABOUT ORIN:

He's in his twenties.
He's highly intelligent.
He's interested in spirituality.
He's intrigued by church.
He has a great sense of humor.
He's respectful of other
people's ideas.
HE'S BEEN TREATED LIKE HE'S
AN IDIOT BY QUITE A
FEW CHRISTIANS.

I met Orin in Barnes & Noble a few weeks ago. He was reading a book on spirituality. He's a gaming developer. He started the conversation because he overheard me talking about helping students find a calling and vocation.

Just in case you haven't noticed, the planet is getting crowded with people who are not like you. ↓

WELCOME TO 98118.

That's the zip code for Columbia City, Washington. It's southeast of Seattle and considered to be one of the most diverse spots in the United States according to the last census. Within six square miles, there are nearly 40,000 people who speak at least 59 different languages.

A study of 98118 can teach us how to live in a world that is increasingly complex, and how to love people who don't agree with us.

By the way, people who are not like you are still like you.

I hope this doesn't bother you. But I have to say it. People who don't share your religious or political views have more in common with you than you may think.
They have **emotions**.
They get **sick**.
They have **jobs**.
They are in **relationships**.
They have **families**.
They **know Harry**.
They want a **better future**.

So get ready, the world is getting closer in a lot of ways.
Urbanization has
transformed communities.

According to the World Bank,

This is the first time in human history that the majority of the world's population lives in urban areas. 3.3 billion people—more than half the world's population—live in cities... Almost 180,000 people move into cities each day.[1]

Here's an idea. What if the complexity of our culture is

irreversible? Instead of spending energy trying to create a culture where people look and think like we do, we should spend some effort learning how to get along with those who are different. For the most part people like living in diversity. At the same time there seems to be a growing dislike toward groups who are
critical
insensitive
or **intolerant** of those who are different than them.

PEOPLE ARE EMBRACING DIVERSITY AND REJECTING THOSE WHO SHOW SIGNS OF INTOLERANCE.

Prejudice is going out-of-style. Maybe not everywhere, but anti-prejudice is becoming a positive trend in a lot of places. I'm personally glad it's not in vogue to be biased toward people who are different. But it also means Christians have to rethink how we discuss our faith, values and beliefs. How we say what we say is becoming more important than what

we say. Many of our conversations will not be with people who
think like us
know us or
trust us.

While I was writing this, Kara Powell, director of the Fuller Youth Institute, reminded me of 1 Peter 3:15: "But in your hearts set apart Christ as Lord. Always be **prepared** to give an answer to **everyone** who **asks** you to give the **reason** for the **hope** that you have. But do this with **gentleness** and respect."

WE COULD SPEND PAGES DISCUSSING THE IMPLICATIONS OF THAT ONE VERSE. ALMOST EVERY WORD RAISES IMPORTANT QUESTIONS WE SHOULD ANSWER.

PREPARED	Are we learning?
EVERYONE	Are we open to people who are different?
ASKS	Are we okay with hard questions?
REASONS	Are we clear about the gospel?
HOPE	Are we positive?
GENTLENESS	Are we caring?
RESPECT	Are we really listening?

MY GOAL IS NOT TO GET PEOPLE TO TRUST ME SO THEY WILL **HEAR** ME, BUT TO LOVE PEOPLE IN SUCH A WAY THEY WILL **ASK** ME. WHAT PEOPLE FEEL SAFE TO ASK MAY BE DETERMINED BY HOW MUCH THEY KNOW YOU CARE ABOUT THEM.

I'm convinced more than ever Christians should not only be the first to engage in conversations with those who are different, but we should also be the first to pursue deeper friendships. According to 1 Peter, my goal is not to get people to trust me so they will hear me, but to love people in such a way they will ask me. What people feel safe to ask you may be determined by how much they know you care.

LOVE YOUR NEIGHBOR AS YOURSELF.

**LEARN HOW TO BECOME
A 98118 NEIGHBOR.**

There are going to be more opportunities to practice "loving" your neighbor than there have ever been. Don't forget Jesus did actually say, "Love your neighbor as yourself." In fact, Jesus was talking about neighbors long before Mr. Rogers or State Farm. You should also know, in case you missed it, the Son of God made this idea a pretty big one. It came right after the "Love the Lord your God" commandment. He made it such a big deal that one of the Pharisees got nervous and asked Him to define the term *neighbor*.

SO, TWO THOUSAND YEARS AGO, JESUS RE-DEFINED THE IDEA OF "NEIGHBOR" FOREVER.

HE TOLD A STORY ABOUT HOW A SAMARITAN HELPED SOMEONE WHO WAS JEWISH.

NOW THAT'S A GAME-CHANGER.

It's simple.

 Go be a neighbor to someone who is different from you.

HERE ARE A FEW NEIGHBORLY TIPS TO REMEMBER.

BE WHO YOU ARE.
You are a follower of Jesus Christ. So be one. Your goal isn't to blend in, neither is it to unnecessarily offend. But be a distinctive believer, not an egotistical believer. Authenticity goes a long way.

DON'T TRY TO CHANGE WHO THEY ARE.
Jesus didn't say, "Change your neighbor as yourself."

**DECIDE TO BE HER FRIEND,
EVEN IF SHE NEVER BECOMES A CHRISTIAN.**
I actually had a friend of our family ask me if I would still be her friend if she never became a Christian. It was a game-changer for both of us.

RESPECT THEIR IDEAS.
Chances are, some of your neighbors are smarter than you. I know that may be hard to believe.
Be careful not to act ... like you know something you don't, or like you know something *they* don't.
It's okay to disagree in the right way. Disagreement just gives you a great opportunity to prove you're really a friend.

HAVE FUN LIKING THEM.
It's okay. You have officially been given permission to like them, and not make them the enemy. (Oh, in case you do think of them as your enemy, Jesus said you should love your enemies too—Luke 6:27-36.)

Here's another interesting statistic: Almost 60 percent of Americans say they want to live in a place where people have several different religions, while 25 percent would rather live mostly with people of the same religion.[2]

Not only are communities becoming more diverse, more people like to live in communities that are diverse. Do you wonder who the 25 percent are who don't want to live in a community with people from different religions? I hope none of these are Christians. Shouldn't most Christians *want* to be around people who are different?

Sometimes it seems the way we build churches reflects the sentiment that we don't.

Most people will acknowledge that the unchurched come from a variety of backgrounds. Yet, most church strategies for intentionally reaching the unchurched in a particular community seem to be cookie-cutter approaches originating in areas that may have little in common with the church's community[3] (Thom Rainer).

ALMOST 60 PERCENT OF AMERICANS SAY THEY WANT TO LIVE IN A PLACE WHERE PEOPLE HAVE SEVERAL DIFFERENT RELIGIONS,

WHILE 25 PERCENT WOULD RATHER LIVE MOSTLY WITH PEOPLE OF THE SAME RELIGION.

YOU DON'T HAVE TO BE LIKE SOMEONE TO LIKE SOMEONE.

I actually like Orin. I've learned I don't have to be like someone to like them. If I were being honest I would admit that I like Orin better than some Christians I know. He's a lot nicer. But I probably shouldn't say that.

A good friend of mine who moved into an urban area recently confessed something similar. He said, "The church convinced me for years that I was supposed to *love* people who are different, but they never gave me permission to *like* people who are different. I've given myself permission to do that, and I'm enjoying it."

This is a great time to be alive. The disciples took Jesus seriously when He said, "Go into all the world and make disciples." They left and went. At some point, those early Christians had to stop acting like an insulated Old Testament Hebrew tribe and start acting like inclusive New Testament believers. The world is moving next door to your office, house or community. Will you be a good neighbor?

"THE CHURCH CONVINCED ME FOR YEARS THAT I WAS SUPPOSED TO LOVE PEOPLE WHO ARE DIFFERENT, BUT THEY NEVER GAVE ME PERMISSION TO LIKE PEOPLE WHO ARE DIFFERENT."

IT'S YOUR TURN: COLLABORATE

WHAT STEPS CAN YOUR CHURCH TAKE TO BEGIN TO
BUILD A BRIDGE TO A GROUP OF PEOPLE WHO ARE
DIFFERENT THAN THOSE WHO ATTEND YOUR CHURCH?

HERE ARE SOME IDEAS
ADD YOUR OWN

PERSONALIZE IT
FOR YOU

Intentionally build a personal relationship with someone whose cultural background or beliefs are (very) different from yours.

STRATEGIZE IT
WITH YOUR TEAM

Visit and network with churches of a different demographic to learn from each other.

ORANGIFY IT
FOR THE NEXT GENERATION

Volunteer at a local public school. Consider adopting a disadvantaged school that needs support or assistance.

LEARN TO BE A GOOD NEIGHBOR IN A COMPLEX CULTURE

SUNDAYS ARE FOR FOOTBALL

RE-IMAGINE WAYS CHURCH CAN INFLUENCE ACTIVE COMMUNITIES

3

King James I issued a three-page pamphlet in 1618. It was called *The Book of Sports*, and it enumerated Sunday recreations—including mixed dancing, archery and ale-drinking—that were lawful "after the end of divine service."[1]

Maybe that's why the NFL waits until Sundays at 1 p.m. to start playing their games.

Evidently, playing sports on Sunday has been a tradition for quite a while. I noticed it first-hand a few weeks ago. I was driving from L.A. to San Diego after speaking at a church on a Sunday morning. The parks were packed with families, the fields with soccer players, the malls with shoppers, and In-N-Out Burger with meat eaters. There were people everywhere.

Then it suddenly dawned on me:

None of these people had gone to church that morning.
Maybe it was because they had not realized I was speaking.
Maybe it was because they had previous commitments.
But their priorities were definitely not in the right place.

THEY OBVIOUSLY HAD NEVER READ KING JAMES' *BOOK OF SPORTS!*

Maybe they read this opening kickoff report from *USA Today*: "It's time. Time for pro-football fans to once again worship at modern-day cathedrals known as stadiums. Time to gather in homage to that autumnal sporting rite—the first Sunday of the NFL season."[2]

WILL YOU BE REALLY HONEST FOR A MINUTE?

Do you ever feel like the church is losing the Sunday war?

If you stop to think about the number of people who are walking away on who never show up to church, it can be overwhelming.

Personally, I get this sinking feeling most people don't want to go to church on Sunday mornings.

> IT'S NOT THAT PEOPLE DON'T LOVE SUNDAYS. EVERYBODY LOVES SUNDAY.

At some point on the sacred day, they will be playing, napping, drinking, golfing, hanging, reading, sunning, swimming, Web-surfing, or watching football.

That is, unless they have to work. (Which, 35 percent will have to do every weekend.)

Statistically, 25 percent of Americans treat Sunday like a Holy Day. Everybody else treats Sunday like a holiday.

The point is, everybody who knows Harry loves Sundays.

The problem is most people don't love church.

It's not that they hate church. They just don't think about church.

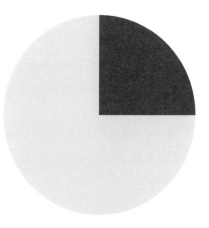

STATISTICALLY, 25 PERCENT OF AMERICANS TREAT SUNDAY LIKE A HOLY DAY.

EVERYBODY ELSE TREATS SUNDAY LIKE A HOLIDAY.

The Bureau of Labor Statistics says, "40 percent of us socialize on Sundays, but twice as many—eight out of 10—sit back and watch TV for an average of four hours. And then there's church: one in four attends religious services. And about that same number goes shopping."[3]

It could be that the same people who are going to church are actually the ones shopping—at least that would explain why tithing is down!

JUST PICK THE FOLLOWING STATISTIC FROM THE RESEARCHER YOU LIKE BEST

The kids who are growing up in church are walking away from church after high school at alarming rates.

Fuller says 50%
Barna says 59%
Lifeway says 70%

ROBERT PUTNAM, the author of *Bowling Alone* and *American Grace,* says the shift is cataclysmic. Young people are dropping out of religion with astounding speed, five times the historical average. As many as 30 to 40 percent say they have no religious affiliation. That number was 5 or 10 percent only a generation ago.[4]

DAVID KINNAMAN says, "Young people are dropping out earlier, staying away longer, and if they come back are less likely to see the church as a long-term part of their life."[5]

DAVID OLSON claims, "The vast majority of churches in America (roughly 80 percent) are in a state of decline. If present trends continue, the percentage of the population that attends church in 2050 is estimated to be at almost half of 1990s attendance—a drop from 20.4 percent to 11.7 percent." Olson's projections for the years leading up to 2050 aren't any more encouraging. He estimates a drop to 15.4 percent in the next eight years.[6]

So, what's the problem?
Why the drop-out rate?
The answers are complex.
There are a lot
of unsettling rumors.

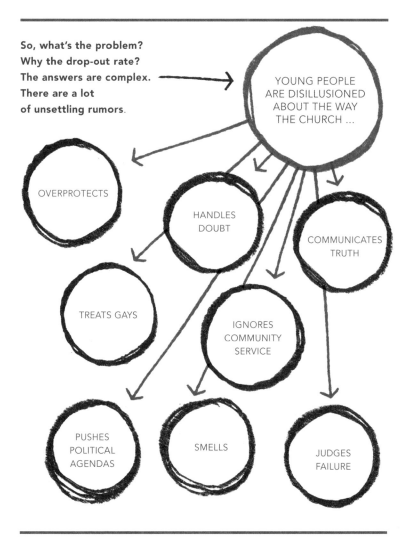

YOUNG PEOPLE
ARE DISILLUSIONED
ABOUT THE WAY
THE CHURCH ...

OVERPROTECTS

HANDLES
DOUBT

COMMUNICATES
TRUTH

TREATS GAYS

IGNORES
COMMUNITY
SERVICE

PUSHES
POLITICAL
AGENDAS

SMELLS

JUDGES
FAILURE

I'M GOING TO OVERSIMPLIFY
AND SAY I THINK IT'S BECAUSE 75
PERCENT OF THE POPULATION
HAS DECIDED

SUNDAY IS FOR FOOTBALL ...
OR FUN
OR FAMILY
OR FRIENDS

HERE ARE THE REASONS JEN DOESN'T GO TO CHURCH. SHE STOPPED GOING WHEN SHE WAS IN HIGH SCHOOL.

- I feel like they're judging me.
- It's usually not on my radar.
- I find more acceptance other places.
- They seem to vilify people, especially young people.
- I feel marginalized, not valuable.
- I have to work on Sundays.
- I have concerns about their rules.
- My questions aren't answered.
- They discriminate against
- my friends.
- I don't like someone yelling at me, it's not my style.
- It doesn't feel like it's worth my time.
- I just don't enjoy the experience.
- I don't know anyone.
- I don't trust their agenda.
- No one invites me to go with them.

BUT SHE ALSO SAID … "IF A FRIEND INVITED ME, I'D GO."

For whatever reason, most people are not going to your church this Sunday.

COMMUNITIES HAVE SHIFTED AWAY FROM A SUNDAYS-ARE-FOR-CHURCH MINDSET

So, what do you do?
Here are some options:

a. **Get Congress to re-instate King James' rule for mandatory church.**
b. **Add a contemporary service at 8:30 a.m.**
c. **Do a weekly simulcast with Bono and Oprah.**
d. **Preach longer in-depth expository messages.**
e. **Re-imagine new ways to connect with people who aren't coming to church.**

Can I pause here for a minute to clarify something?

I don't think most churches should simply stop what they are doing.

Twenty-five percent of people are coming. A lot of churches are doing great work with a host of people. And a lot of people are happy about it.

Take me for example.
I go to a BIG church. I always have. I love big churches. I always will. There is something about the energy, a crowd singing, the big screen, and an inspiring message that moves me. And I'm not planning on losing my faith anytime soon.
Take my friend John, for example.
He goes to a SMALL church. He always has. He loves small churches. He always will. There is something about the intimacy, the old hymns, the big pulpit, and the fact that everybody knows his name that moves him.

We both love our churches.
And people who love church need churches they love.
All 25 percent of us.

I'm just wondering about the rest of the people.

THE 75 PERCENT.

Not the people who will show up at church one day.
But the people who will NEVER show up.
Either they left or they never came to begin with.

Don't miss this shift.
25% of people will be in Church Sunday—the rest think Sundays are for football.

What if you stopped counting the people who come to your church every Sunday and started counting the people in your community who don't?

Don't count those who *attend*.
Count those who are absent.

What are we going to do about them?
We are great at doing church for people who already go to church, and even for those who will go one day.
But what can we do to connect with the people who will never go?

WHAT IF YOU STOPPED COUNTING THE PEOPLE WHO COME TO YOUR CHURCH EVERY SUNDAY AND STARTED COUNTING THE PEOPLE IN YOUR COMMUNITY WHO DON'T

Those who think Sunday is for football.
The 15 percent who check "none"
for religious preference.
(It's up from eight percent in 1990)[7]
The 35 percent who have to work or
travel on Sundays.
The 75 percent who will never
have a desire to walk into a
building on a bright Sunday
morning to listen to a band or
choir and a 40-minute sermon.

If Jesus said leave the 99 to go
find the one, maybe we can stop
thinking about the 25 long enough
to brainstorm ideas to reach the 75.

Have we forgotten how to
be missionaries in our own
communities?

Every Sunday, we pass people who
will never go to church with us or
anybody else.

Is our primary goal to get them to
come to a building from nine to
noon on Sunday?
Is their only invitation to the Gospel
going to happen because we ask
them to stand up in front of a room
filled with strangers?

What if church, the way we have
defined it, will never work for them?
It may work for 25 out of 100,
but what about the rest?
As far as they are concerned,
Sundays are for football.

So, we need to re-imagine ways to
play our game.

neighborhood events
unconventional groups
online churches
community efforts
family experiences

**CHANGE ANYTHING.
TRY EVERYTHING,
UNTIL YOU FIND SOMETHING
THAT WORKS.**

To reach people no one else is
reaching we must do things no one
else is doing, **Craig Groeschel**.

There are ways of doing church that
no one has thought of yet. If we
keep trying to meet new challenges
with tired old ideas, I'm afraid we'll
fade into irrelevant oblivion,
Mark Batterson.

IT'S YOUR TURN: COLLABORATE

HOW ARE YOU GOING TO CONNECT WITH THE PEOPLE IN YOUR COMMUNITY WHO WILL NEVER STEP INSIDE YOUR BUILDING?

HERE ARE SOME IDEAS
ADD YOUR OWN

PERSONALIZE IT
FOR YOU

STRATEGIZE IT
WITH YOUR TEAM

ORANGIFY IT
FOR THE NEXT
GENERATION

Invest relationally in someone who doesn't go to church. Everyone needs someone to remind them how people who don't go to church think.

Create new opportunities outside Sunday morning services to engage people who don't go to church. It's okay to experiment.

Host an interactive experience for families (FX) for the community.

RE-IMAGINE WAYS CHURCH CAN INFLUENCE ACTIVE COMMUNITIES

THEY BLEW UP WALNUT GROVE

WAKE UP TO THE REALITY OF TODAY'S COMPLICATED FAMILY

4

American homes a heart-warming glimpse of how family life looked for a farming community between the late 1860s and 1880s.

Families worked together
lived together
prayed together
went to church together
stayed together
and *slept in bonnets.*

Michael Landon said "I believe in God, family, truth between people, the power of love."[1]

It sounds simple. It was obviously the philosophy behind his series, *The Little House on the Prairie,* that aired on NBC between 1974 and 1984.

For 10 seasons, Landon's adaptation of Laura Ingalls' famous books gave

We love to idolize and idealize the way things were.
But here's the irony.
While I sat with my Boomer parents in our den on Monday nights and watched a romanticized traditional version of family, the families around us were evolving into something very different.

A number of experts point to the 70s and 80s as a major turning

"I BELIEVE IN GOD, FAMILY, TRUTH BETWEEN PEOPLE, THE POWER OF LOVE."
MICHAEL LANDON

point for the home. Just before and during the years *Little House* aired, our country had begun to radically redefine family life.

REMEMBER THOSE YEARS?

Martin Luther King Jr., *Sesame Street*, Woodstock, Moon landing, Vietnam, Watergate, sexual revolution, Roe vs. Wade, RCA Color Television, Equal Rights Amendment, no-fault divorce, Moral Majority, Nintendo. And in 1982, the term AIDS was used for the first time.

Lists like this raise a wide range of emotions for those of us who grew up with mood rings and lava lamps.

Leaders at Stanford University summarize the period this way:

This fundamental social institution (of the family) has changed profoundly since 1980. In fact, if one were to define the most original demographic feature in the post-1980 period in the United States, it would be the changes that were occurring in both families and households for all

sections of the national population. The traditional American family has been undergoing profound transformations for all ages, all races, and all ethnic groups.[2]

On February 6, 1984, Michael Landon made the decision to blow up Walnut Grove. In this final episode, "The Last Farewell," the characters blew up the buildings of their town because a railroad tycoon had acquired the rights to their land. They were making a statement about progress:

"YOU CAN TAKE OUR LAND, BUT YOU CAN NEVER HAVE OUR TOWN!"

According to Landon, the buildings were destroyed during the filming to make sure no other productions would ever be made on the set of "Walnut Grove." On one hand he seemed to suggest, "The ideals of *Little House* need to be preserved forever." While on the other hand he implied, "You can never go back."

Blowing up Walnut Grove sent a subtle but profound message to a generation.

"Don't romanticize the ideals of the past so much that you miss the story of the present."

Or stated another way,

"Don't get so obsessed with trying to go back to the way things were you can't live with the way things are!"

So, maybe it's smart to blow up Walnut Grove.

There are a host of leaders who want to re-create a *Little House on the Prairie* version of the family.

The problem is most of the families they are called to reach have no context for a family that looks like the Ingalls.

If you are hoping to find a culture where ...

Only men make the decisions

Girls have to learn sewing

Everybody looks the same

Most people live to be only 45

Plumbing is outdoors

Relational conflicts and tragedies are resolved in an hour

with a verse from the Bible ...

You're not going to find it.

AND FAMILIES TODAY NEED HOPE.

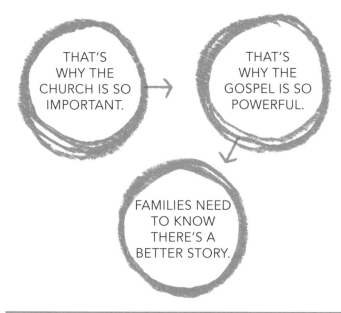

THAT'S WHY THE CHURCH IS SO IMPORTANT.

THAT'S WHY THE GOSPEL IS SO POWERFUL.

FAMILIES NEED TO KNOW THERE'S A BETTER STORY.

GOD DESIGNED THE FAMILY. HE'S HAD A PLAN SINCE THE BEGINNING TO USE BROKEN FAMILIES TO DEMONSTRATE HIS STORY OF REDEMPTION.

It's simply not the reality of today's family.

Don't fall into a trap as a leader. Whenever you try to lead families to an unrealistic ideal:
Your leaders will start to feel helpless.
Your parents will start to feel hopeless.

HERE'S A QUICK
THEOLOGICAL PERSPECTIVE.

Every family is broken
Those who go to church
Those who don't
Those who are married
Those who aren't
Those who believe like you
Those who can't

The truth is, the family was broken long before Walnut Grove ever blew up. Remember Eden?

The story of a perfect man and a perfect woman.
They were literally made for each other. If any couple ever had a chance for a perfect family, it would have been Adam and Eve.
But that's not how the story goes. Things got complicated fast. Since then, the family has been on a roller coaster ride. It has navigated through the practice of polygamy, arranged marriages, concubines, abuse, science, technology and a host of political debates.

REMEMBER THIS:
THERE HAS NEVER BEEN
ONE FAMILY THAT DIDN'T
NEED GRACE.

Your job isn't to get every family back to Walnut Grove, or even Eden. Your job is to help EVERY family understand, regardless of their history, baggage or present situation, that they are invited into a bigger story of restoration and redemption.

God designed the family.
He's had a plan since the beginning to use broken families to demonstrate His story of redemption.
(By the way: He has the same plan for using broken people to be the church.)

So, **blow up Walnut Grove**.
It's time to wake up to a new reality of family.

MOST HOMES TODAY REFLECT NON-TRADITIONAL FAMILIES WHO STRUGGLE TO CONNECT WITH THE CHRISTIAN COMMUNITY.

Remember, you are not called to live in the past, but to lead something now. You can't go back to *Little House on the Prairie*. It doesn't mean you have to agree with everything that is happening. But it does mean you may need to let go of unrealistic pictures today's families can't live up to.

While Michael Landon was blowing up Walnut Grove, the first wave of Millennials were playing in preschool.
They were the children born between 1980 and 2000.

They are presently the 12- to 32-year-olds in your church and community.
They represent many of the kids, teenagers and parents you are called to influence.

HERE ARE SOME OF THE PRIMARY TRENDS THAT ARE REDEFINING THE REALITY OF THEIR FAMILY EXPERIENCE.

More of them are:
- getting married later
- living together without getting married
- unmarried couples raising children
- gay and lesbian couples raising children
- single women having children without a male partner to help
- parents who will adopt children.
- mothers of young children working outside the home
- raising children with special-needs
- marrying people of a different race
- living with extended families

So, are you wondering which of these things I approve or disapprove?
I bet you are! At this point, I'm just saying this is the new reality.
A lot has changed since the Boomer and Buster years.

CONSIDER SOME OF THE FOLLOWING STATS.

In **1960**, **59%** of those who were 18-29 were married.
In **2010**, **20%** of those who were age 18-29 were married.[3]

In **1950**, **16%** of women with children under 18 worked outside the home.
In **1960**, **35%** of women with children under 18 worked outside the home.[4]
In **2009**, **71.4%** of women with children under 18 worked outside the home.[5]

In the early **1960**s, **four or five children** in **10,000** were affected with autism.
Today, **one** in every **100** children are affected.[6]
One in five households have at least one child with special healthcare needs.[7]

In **1960**, **2.5%** of new marriages were interracial.
In **2010**, **15%** of new marriages were interracial.[8]

In **1940**, **25%** lived with multi-generational family.
In **1980**, **12%** lived with multi-generational family.
In **2008**, **16%** lived with multi-generational family[9]

In **1962**, **272,000** children were in foster care.[10]
In **2010**, **408,425** children were in foster care.
and **107,000** children were waiting to be adopted. [11]

1970, **11%** of children lived in mother-only families.
In **2011**, **24%** of children lived in mother-only families.[12]
And **26%** of children lived in single-parent homes.[13]

In **1988**, **11%** of Americans approved of same-sex marriage.
In **2010**, **46%** of Americans approve of same-sex marriage.[14]
(**21%** of those who are over 65 support same-sex marriage.)
(**55%** of those who are 18-29 support same-sex marriage.) [15]

In the **1960**s, **10%** of couples lived together before marriage.
Today, **65%** live together before marriage.[16]

In **1980**, **18.4%** of births were to unmarried women.[17]
In **2007**, nearly **40%** of all births were to unmarried women.[18]
Today, **63%** of births to women under 30 occur outside marriage.[19]

In **1960**, **one** in **100** children lived with a parent who had never been married.
In **2010**, **one** in **10** children live with a parent who has never been married.[20]

So, guess what?
You have an incredible opportunity to invest in kids whose parents are
interracial
married, remarried, or never married at all
adoptive
divorced or single
gay or straight.

Have you ever considered—
Children will decide what they think about the church when they see how you treat their parents.

CHILDREN WILL DECIDE WHAT THEY THINK ABOUT THE CHURCH WHEN THEY SEE HOW YOU TREAT THEIR PARENTS.

WHY DO I THINK THAT?
IN HIS BOOK *MILLENNIALS*, THOM RAINER ASKS AN OPEN-ENDED QUESTION TO THIS AGE GROUP.

 WHAT IS REALLY IMPORTANT IN YOUR LIFE?
Here are the top five responses:

61% FAMILY
25% FRIENDS
17% EDUCATION
16% CAREER
13% SPOUSE/PARTNER[21]

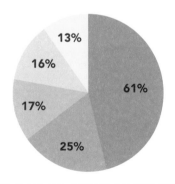

Church didn't even make it on the list.
And nothing on the list is even a close second to family.

RESEARCH INDICATES THAT MILLENNIALS HAVE A BETTER ATTITUDE TOWARD THEIR FAMILY THAN THEY DO THE CHURCH. IT ALSO SUGGESTS THEY CARE ABOUT EVERY FAMILY BETTER THAN THE CHURCH DOES.

THAT'S WHY IT SHOULD BE A PRIORITY FOR CHURCHES TO BUILD A BRIDGE TO A VARIETY OF FAMILIES, TO ALL FAMILIES, IN THEIR COMMUNITIES.

THAT'S WHY CHRISTIAN LEADERS NEED TO DISCOVER NEW WAYS TO RESPOND TO THE COMPLICATED ISSUES FACING THIS GENERATION'S FAMILIES.

So, let's take the elephant in the room and put it on the table.

Here are some of the questions I hear leaders ask behind closed doors.

Will you do a baby dedication for a child whose parents are cohabitating? Do you believe someone gay can attend your church and pursue a relationship with God? Can children of gay couples participate in your ministries and programs? Can any parent attend your parenting training or classes? What is your strategy for a couple in your church who gets divorced? How are you inviting families in your church to participate in helping the orphans and widows of this generation? (That includes those who need foster care, adoption, and parents who are single without support of a spouse.) Will you do premarital counseling for couples who live together? Will you do their wedding? Can they join your church? What is your plan when a teenager in your church finds out they are pregnant, or they have been abused, or they think they're gay? What services will you provide for children with special needs? How do you plan to encourage and support their parents?

CHRISTIAN LEADERS NEED TO DISCOVER NEW WAYS TO RESPOND TO THE COMPLICATED ISSUES FACING THIS GENERATION'S FAMILIES

Do I have answers? Maybe, but I'm not going to tell you.
I'm not sure anyone else should script these answers for you or your church.

You should obviously look at what Scripture says.

But don't expect it to give you a script for every scenario.
It's a compass, not a GPS.
Today's family is complicated.
And this generation needs you to care enough to personally wrestle with their issues.

But before you start making any policy, consider:
How you discuss these issues may be more important than how you answer.

Again, here's another way to say it.
Parents will decide what they think about the church, when they see how you treat their families.

Most of this generation gets their impression of the church from picket signs, Bible bytes and the media. What they really need are leaders who will sit down across a table from them who care enough to hear their story ... and who will help them move their family toward a better story.

LITTLE HOUSE IS GONE. MODERN FAMILY IS HERE. THINGS ARE COMPLICATED.

TODAY'S FAMILY IS COMPLICATED.

IT'S YOUR TURN: COLLABORATE

HOW WILL YOU DO MINISTRY FOR THE GROWING
NUMBER OF NON-TRADITIONAL FAMILIES IN YOUR
COMMUNITY?

HERE ARE SOME IDEAS
ADD YOUR OWN

PERSONALIZE IT
FOR YOU

Pick a non-traditional family category you don't understand and learn about it (special needs, single parents, blended families, co-habitation, gay parents).

STRATEGIZE IT
WITH YOUR TEAM

Establish focus groups of non-traditional families to help you understand their concerns and needs. Create a clear strategy to encourage families who are candidates for foster care and adoption, and families who have children with special needs.

ORANGIFY IT
FOR THE NEXT GENERATION

Maximize resources and special events to help parents in your community win at home. (parent workshops, milestone events: baby dedicaton, service opportunities, online resources, ParentCue mobile app, etc.).

WAKE UP TO THE REALITY OF TODAY'S COMPLICATED FAMILY

ZOMBIES ARE EASY TO LEAD

TREAT THE PEOPLE WHO FOLLOW YOU LIKE HUMANS

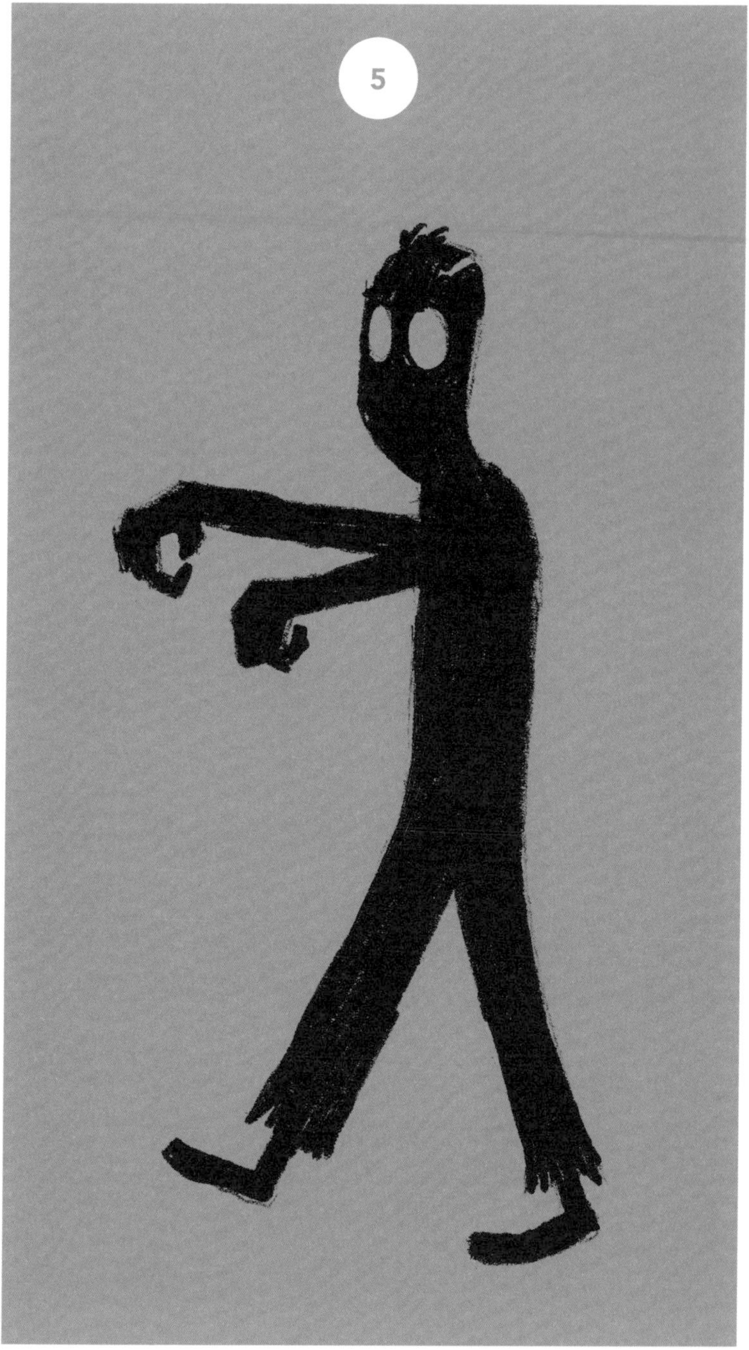

I believe in Zombies. There are a lot of leaders who do. They may not admit it but they often act like there should be creatures who—
follow them without thinking
follow them anywhere
and **follow** them regardless.

That's why so many leaders never listen to your ideas, never care where they lead you and never show respect.

Why should they,
If you're just a zombie?

These leaders make a number of assumptions.
They think they can—
out-run zombies since they are slower.
out-smart zombies since they are dumber.
out-do zombies since they are inferior.
It happens all the time.
Leaders give themselves a false sense of authority
by developing an attitude of superiority.

When leaders make the mistake of leading humans like zombies, they risk alienating a generation of humans that are motivated by something more complicated than their natural impulses to survive. ↓

THAT'S WHY IT'S VITAL FOR LEADERS TO START TREATING HUMANS LIKE HUMANS.

HUMANS WHO HAVE **EMOTIONS**.

HUMANS WHO HAVE **FUTURES**.

HUMANS WHO ARE MADE TO **REASON**, **CREATE**, **INNOVATE**, **DESIGN** AND **THINK**.

PEOPLE ARE CRAVING A DIFFERENT BREED OF LEADER.

LEADERS SHOULD START TREATING THEM LIKE PEOPLE WHO HAVE BRAINS INSTEAD OF CREATURES WHO EAT BRAINS.

LEADERS ARE BEING CALLED TO MODEL A NEW STANDARD OF AUTHENTICITY AND EMPATHY.

So, how is "leading people like they are humans" a game-changer? Just listen to the news. People are craving a different breed of leader. Too many have been burned by bad leaders over the past few years. Now, suddenly their emotional radars are tuned in.

They can easily spot a leader who is
FAKE
SELF-ABSORBED
GREEDY
CONTROLLING
INSECURE
OR INDIFFERENT.

That's why it's a game-changer.

Where are the real leaders who understand they're leading real people?

For me, this game-changer isn't just cultural; it's personal.
A few years ago I heard Patrick Lencioni speak to leaders.
He said something like this,
"My dad would have been a better father if he had worked for a better manager. Don't underestimate the potential your leadership has on the people who work for you."

That day I relived what it was like working on staff with Andy Stanley. Developing leaders is embedded in the culture of North Point Community Church.

Andy invested countless hours in an inner circle of leaders. He respected our opinions, guarded our relationships, and helped us win professionally and personally. He also had to deal with my introverted, creative and impulsive personality for over a decade.

After hearing Lencioni, I felt compelled to make a list of things Andy did for me as a young husband, parent and leader. I still keep it on file to remind me how I should treat those who work on staff at Orange. I've even given it to other senior pastors when they ask what it was like to work for Andy.

Andy acted like his time with us each week was the most important part of his job as a leader. He made his core team a priority. And because of that, we became better leaders.

I have never regarded myself as a great husband or father. But I'm absolutely sure I'm a better husband and father because I had Andy as a leader.

Every time you consider a staff member you lead, remember the way you lead them will impact:
the people they lead
their spouse and their children
their future.

Zombies will follow you anywhere despite what you do.

BUT TALENTED AND PASSIONATE PEOPLE FOLLOW LEADERS WHO TREAT THEM LIKE HUMANS.

MY DAD WOULD HAVE BEEN A BETTER FATHER IF HE HAD WORKED FOR A BETTER MANAGER.

Summarizing helps me stay focused on what's important sometimes. After reading hundreds of leadership books, I narrowed it down to a few things.

I THINK THE PEOPLE I LEAD WANT ME TO

1	2	3	4	5
Care about their future.	Value their talents.	Respect their ideas.	Make good decisions.	Do something that matters.

What if every leader simply decided to focus on people? I sense a new commitment among leaders to establish a higher standard when it comes to valuing and serving the people they lead.

When Starbucks was faced with a difficult decision to cut $600 million to survive, founder Howard Schultz made a hard choice. The company could save $320 million with one single move: drop the generous, groundbreaking health care program that gives benefits even to part-time employees. Schultz refused, saying the benefits were as much a part of the Starbucks culture as the coffee itself. Two years later, Starbucks stock has tripled in price.[1]

Mattel wanted to keep in touch with its main customers: kids. So, every

Friday at 1 p.m., the biggest toy company in the world closes early so employees have playtime and can take paid time off to volunteer in local schools.[2]

Talk about a magical cobbler. Online shoe giant Zappos gives every employee $50 to award as a bonus to another employee—every single month. Then the bonus-ees are eligible to be the monthly Hero, complete with a cape and a parade to the tune of "I Need a Hero."[3]

I know what you're thinking: *It's all just part of the image game of corporate America, trying to redeem their reputations.* Maybe I'm naïve, but I have met incredible business leaders over the past years who seem authentic in their attempts to make people a priority.

Laszlo Bock, Google's innovative Senior Vice President for Human Resources, told the *New York Times*:

If I'm a manager and I want to get better, and I want more out of my people and I want them to be happier, two of the most important things I can do is to just make sure I have some time for them and to be consistent. And that's more important than doing the rest of the stuff.

In his book *Good to Great: Why Some Companies Make the Leap*, Jim Collins makes this observation:

The people we interviewed from the good-to-great companies clearly loved what they did, largely because they loved who they did it with.[5]

That's why the average leader should stop treating people like zombies.

Of course, Christian leaders would never treat humans like zombies. They treat people like sheep. Don't overanalyze that too much.

Shouldn't Christian leaders be the first in line to study leadership principles and become excellent at what they do?
It seems like if we really believe our mission is critical, we should be reading everything we can to become better leaders.

CHRISTIANS CAN AND SHOULD LEARN FROM A VARIETY OF LEADERS.

LET'S CHASE A RABBIT FOR A MINUTE.

I realize some people object to learning about leadership principles from non-Christian leaders. I agree that a lot of principles used in a corporate setting should not be practiced in the church. But, I also definitely think Christians can and should learn from a variety of leaders—even those who may not be Christians. Why?

Pick any one of the following reasons:

A. God created gifted leaders to teach the rest of us.
B. Leaders in the church are responsible to lead well too.
C. Some of the best leadership advice is actually biblical.
D. All of the above.

I think the answer is "d. All of the above." I learned that from John Maxwell, who happens to be a leading game-changer for leaders.

I've always wondered why Christian leaders who reject the advice of non-Christian leaders will still take advice from a non-Christian golf pro.

Really? Do you think it's more important for a pastor to get better at golf, OR BETTER AT LEADING?

Most of us were *called* to lead the church. None of us were *called* to play golf.

BUT HERE'S WHAT I BELIEVE:
Jesus is in charge, and
He calls people to be leaders.
He gave us a mission, so what we are leading is important.
He wants leaders to lead the church to take His gospel to the world.
  ... And golfing is not biblical.

That's okay. I'm not saying golfing is bad. I'm just saying it's not in the Bible. I didn't say it was anti-biblical.
It's just non-biblical.
But so are air-conditioning, football, toilet paper, McDonald's, movies, some worship songs, Google, Facebook and Harry.

Wine is biblical.
Ask the Episcopals.
Chick-fil-A is biblical.
Genesis says, "God created ... every winged bird after its kind."

WHAT'S THE POINT?
Everything that's in the Bible is true.
Everything that's not in the Bible is not bad.
There are some things not in the Bible that might be good for you to know. Think about that while you tweet ... or golf.

Oh yeah. Weren't we talking about non-biblical leadership?
This game-changing idea about zombie leadership really is in the Bible. No. I'm not claiming zombies are biblical, although I'm pretty sure Lazarus looked the part. But leading people in a loving way *is* biblical.

Here's a quick review of some biblical leaders who had authority. There were prophets, priests, kings, judges, teachers, overseers, ministers, leaders, deacons, pastors, shepherds, missionaries, elders.

It seems like a lot of people were leading in the Bible.
Even women!

Paul was a leader. Remember him? He was called to lead churches. So, he spent most of his life leading leaders to lead churches everywhere.
That's why he pushed Timothy into the spotlight as a young leader.

Anti-Zombie Leadership Principle

LEAD LEADERS LIKE THEY ARE LEADERS.

TREAT PEOPLE YOU'RE LEADING LIKE THEY HAVE AS MUCH POTENTIAL AS YOU. THEY ARE TALENTED LEADERS WHO MAY TAKE YOUR PLACE ONE DAY.

Treat people you're leading like they have as much potential as you.
They are not zombies.
They are talented leaders who may take your place one day.
They are possible Timothys.

So, push them into the spotlight. Treat your volunteers like the potential leaders they probably already are. Your style of leadership, how you respect and empower the people who do ministry with you will determine the kind of leaders you attract. In other words, be careful they never feel like you are trying to "zombify" them.

Think about how God used Paul at a strategic moment in history.
He was responsible for starting and leading churches, mobilizing volunteers, and empowering the next generation.

If Paul was available for an interview on this subject, I think he would have some interesting things to say to leaders. He is an example of why this principle on leadership is so important. His relationship with Timothy illustrates why every leader should focus on developing other's leadership gifts to reproduce

ministry exponentially. Here's some of his advice:

If you want others to follow you, even though you are young, then lead by an example in your speech, in your manners, in how you love, in your faith and in your lifestyle.
(1 Timothy 4:12, RJLT)[6]

That leads us to …

**Anti-Zombie
Leadership Principle**

2

LEAD YOURSELF IF YOU WANT
HUMANS TO FOLLOW.

Show the people you're leading that it's personal.

Yeah, zombies will always follow, but humans may not. They need to be inspired. You have to lead from a life message and a mission that's worth following.

Here's something else Paul said
to Timothy ...

"Don't treat people like zombies,
(okay, not that part, but he did say
what's next)
don't rebuke an older man harshly,
but encourage him as if he were
your father.
Treat younger men as brothers,
older women as mothers,
and younger women as sisters,
[in all purity] with right motives.
(1 Timothy 5:1-2)

That means ...

Anti-Zombie
Leadership Principle

LEAD HUMANS LIKE
THEY ARE HUMANS.

The people you are leading should
be important to you.
You're leading real people,
not zombies.

They are—
HUMAN HUSBANDS AND WIVES
HUMAN SONS AND DAUGHTERS
HUMAN FATHERS AND MOTHERS.

What if you just decided to treat
those you lead like they were your
own dad or mom, your own brother
or sister? Would it make a difference
in how you lead?
(Of course that's assuming you treat
your own family the right way.)

Just remember, "zombification"
can happen whenever people stop
thinking for themselves and become
lethargic due to bad leadership. It's
kind of ironic. If you treat people
like zombies, they can actually
become zombies. Then you'll have
to spend a lot of your time watching
your back, if you don't want to get
eaten alive.

WHAT IF YOU JUST
DECIDED TO TREAT
THOSE YOU LEAD
LIKE THEY WERE YOUR
OWN DAD OR MOM,
YOUR OWN BROTHER
OR SISTER? WOULD IT
MAKE A DIFFERENCE
IN HOW YOU LEAD?

IT'S YOUR TURN: # COLLABORATE

WHAT ARE SOME PRACTICAL STEPS YOU CAN TAKE
TO PREVENT AN EPIDEMIC OF ZOMBIFICATION IN
YOUR CHURCH?

HERE ARE SOME IDEAS
ADD YOUR OWN

PERSONALIZE IT
FOR YOU

Choose a younger leader and personally commit to invest in them.

STRATEGIZE IT
WITH YOUR TEAM

Brainstorm creative ways to help your volunteers win in their personal and professional lives. (They help you win in yours.)

ORANGIFY IT
FOR THE NEXT GENERATION

Sign up for OrangeLeaders.com for free or subscribe to YouLead to connect to a community of leaders and develop leadership skills.

TREAT THE PEOPLE WHO FOLLOW YOU LIKE HUMANS

IMPROV OR DIE

COLLABORATE TO DISCOVER THE BEST IDEAS AND SOLUTIONS

6

WE LOVE TO LOVE PIXAR.

Who else can create a film with an 80-year-old protagonist who appeals to kids and adults alike?

Who else can make us laugh at whatever is lurking in our closets when we turn out the light?

Who else can make us care so deeply about a clownfish or a French rat or a child's toy?

Randy Nelson, Dean of Pixar University, attributes the company's fantastic success at storytelling to an age-old art form:

IMPROV.

At its core, the Pixar team borrows the best techniques of an improv troupe to fuel its process:

To start with, **accept every idea** that's offered.

 IT'S AN INTIMIDATING CONCEPT. BUT NELSON POINTS OUT THAT A "**NO**" IS AN AUTOMATIC DEAD END.

 WHILE A "**YES**" LEADS TO POSSIBILITY. EVEN IF IT'S NOT THE POSSIBILITY YOU FIRST HAD IN MIND.

The second key to improv is just as simple: **Make your partner look good.**

Pixar's policy ditches a "me-centric" approach. Everyone finds the freedom to promote their coworkers because they know their coworkers are out to elevate them. It's about saying, "This is what I've got. What do you have that makes it even better?"[1]

It's not just storytellers who are discovering the value of a team approach.

Google chief Eric Schmidt has taken "collaborate or perish" as the key theme for his company.

Other organizations like IBM and Cisco are dismantling managerial hierarchies, opting for a flattened model that relies on reciprocal relationships. They've realized that no one company, division, or person has the one best avenue to success.[2]

Everyone seems to recognize the value of collaboration.

In the newly released 2012 Innovation Barometer, General Electric notes that a majority of executives believe innovation is key to their success—and 86 percent of them acknowledge that collaboration is the key to innovation.[3]

GAME

THE ART OF COLLABORATION IS REPLACING CONVENTIONAL MODELS OF MANAGEMENT.

CHANGER

Society is more complicated than it has ever been. Resolving complex issues requires a diverse team of creative thinkers. Look around and you can see collaboration everywhere. A team of **medical specialists** and surgeons perform a life-saving operation.

SOCIETY IS MORE COMPLICATED THAN IT HAS EVER BEEN. RESOLVING COMPLEX ISSUES REQUIRES A DIVERSE TEAM OF CREATIVE THINKERS.

FUNCTIONING AS A TEAM IS DIFFICULT. IT REQUIRES CHECKING YOUR EGO AT THE DOOR. IT MEANS THERE IS NO "MOST VALUABLE PLAYER."

A group of **artists** and **technicians** design a breakthrough gaming idea. A crew of **producers** and **filmmakers** make an award-winning movie.

Collaboration is in, and those who master the art tend to win. The problem is: No one teaches you in school how to collaborate. You are actually taught to "do your own work." That's why companies are turning to non-conventional entities like improv groups to improve their collaboration skills.

Functioning as a team is difficult. It requires checking your ego at the door. It means there is no "most valuable player."

It's easier in some ways to be a one-person team. But ultimately, the solutions and ideas generated by one person will simply not be as effective. Ideas that derive from silo-thinking rarely stand up to collective thinking. Something powerful happens when problems are processed and filtered by a talented group.

I have based much of my life and ministry on this idea: "I am not sure I can figure it out, but if I can get the right people in the room, WE can."

My attempt to define collaboration is simple:

Harness the collective talents of a diverse group to figure it out.

It's fascinating to see companies and corporations championing this concept while so many churches and ministries still function primarily in silos, or with hierarchical organizational charts.

I'm not suggesting that churches shouldn't have a clear leadership structure, but the top-down management approach has limitations.

1.

They resist a pied-piper approach in ministry and broaden their leadership bases.

2.

They reject the silo-thinking that keeps children's ministry leaders and student pastors in their separate rooms.

THE SMARTEST CHURCH LEADERS, DON'T JUST *TALK ABOUT TEAM*, THEY AGGRESSIVELY *PRACTICE* TEAM. THEY KNOW IT'S AN IMPROV OR DIE CULTURE. THAT MEANS—

3.

They believe it's important to synchronize efforts in developing a comprehensive strategy from cradle to college.

4.

They invite the next generation to the meeting and let the next generation challenge the process of how things have always been done.

5.

They act like the letters to the Romans and the Corinthians were actually true, when Paul taught early leaders to exercise their different gifts to contribute in the church.

For the sake of the Gospel, we should champion collaboration. We are called to "harness the collective talents of a diverse church to figure it out."

WHAT IS "IT"?
WHATEVER IT TAKES TO RESCUE A BROKEN WORLD WITH THE POWER OF THE GOSPEL.

It may sound like this is a challenge for the church to catch up to what business leaders are discovering about collaboration. In reality, corporations today are simply amplifying the principles of collaboration that God initially designed.

NEHEMIAH collaborated to re-build a city wall.

DISCIPLES collaborated to make more disciples.

MOSES collaborated to build the tabernacle.

PAUL collaborated to take the Gospel to the entire world.

I was thinking about the importance of collaboration on a flight several months ago as I evaluated our Orange staff. They are a team of sixty-plus innovative writers, thinkers, planners, creators, and doers who are devoted to influencing those who influence the next generation. In many ways, we're a family. And like any family, we have just enough dysfunction and diversity to generate creative tension. It's the kind of tension that I've learned is necessary for innovation.

Some staff members have been together nearly a decade, while others have joined within the past few years.

It occurred to me that I'd never had a conversation with everyone in the same room to talk about how we function as a team. Those of us who had history intuitively understood the rules, while others were operating from a different frame of reference. I had assumed everyone was on the same page about the rules of collaboration.

A COLLABORATIVE CULTURE SENDS A MESSAGE THAT THE MISSION OF YOUR ORGANIZATION IS A SHARED RESPONSIBILITY.

SO, I DECIDED TO MAKE A LIST TO HELP THE TEAM ACT MORE LIKE A TEAM. HERE ARE A FEW OF THE PRINCIPLES I WROTE DOWN.

Everybody's Business is Everybody's Business.

Most of the walls that divide our workspace are glass ... not metaphorical glass, actual see-through, floor-to-ceiling glass walls. So, it's easy to see what is happening everywhere. If you work at Orange, you can invite yourself into most of the meetings that are taking place. A collaborative environment has to be intentional to cross-pollinate between departments.

Silo-thinking assumes those within a department don't ever need outside perspectives. It also presumes those outside a team are not responsible for what happens on someone else's team. Both are false. A collaborative culture sends a message that the mission of your organization is a shared responsibility.

Never keep your opinion to yourself.

People tend to hold back their opinion because of one thing.

Fear.

When you give your opinion—

It could cost you some ego.

It could cost you a relationship with a co-worker.

It could cost you time and energy to get involved.

The sobering truth is that it costs your organization more when you don't speak up. When anyone makes a statement to me privately that they were frustrated by another department's decision, I become frustrated too. I always ask, "Why didn't you say something to them sooner? Your opinion may not have made any difference, but then again, it might have. If you don't speak up about things that matter, then everyone loses."

You win whenever you help someone else win.

No one is an expert.

It's what anyone in improv understands: Collaboration is making someone else look better than you. You must be willing to push others into the spotlight, or there will always be a lid on your leadership. I naturally question anyone who tries to make someone else look bad and get disappointed with anyone who doesn't want someone else to look good.

Here's the real test:

DOES IT BOTHER YOU IF SOMEONE LOOKS BETTER THAN YOU?

People don't want to follow leaders who limit their potential. A tricky line exists between manipulating someone so YOU can win, and motivating someone so the TEAM can win.

When you can't honestly celebrate someone else's success—there's a problem.

I'm not sure anyone is such an expert on anything that they can make decisions without input. But collectively, we can make expert decisions. It's dangerous when someone becomes an island. There is just not enough intellect and experience in one person to make the best decisions. This principle suggests that since no one has arrived, everyone needs to keep learning. Sure, we have specialists who have mastered a specific talent or concept, but they need to remember that information and learning is changing rapidly.

When you realize you are not an expert, you—

Don't stop learning.
Don't stop learning from people who know more than you.
Don't stop learning from people who know less than you.
Don't stop learning more of what you think you already know.

5

Ideas don't have a finish line.

The very nature of innovation suggests you have to continue to improv in order to improve what you are doing.

You have to **improv or die**.

If you stop tweaking,
If it becomes good enough,
If things cease to be relevant,
You are in danger of losing influence with someone.

Maybe even with an
entire generation.

Sure, ideas can be finished *temporarily* in order to meet a publication or event deadline. But no idea is really done. Ideas have living potential to grow and improve. If you don't keep watering and nurturing them, they die, and so do you. That's why you have to become intentional about revisiting and revising what you think you have decided. It's one of the key reasons that Orange publishes mostly online; it allows the flexibility to keep innovating our materials.

BUT NO IDEA IS REALLY DONE. IDEAS HAVE LIVING POTENTIAL TO GROW AND IMPROVE. IF YOU DON'T KEEP WATERING AND NURTURING THEM, THEY DIE, AND SO DO YOU. THAT'S WHY YOU HAVE TO BECOME INTENTIONAL ABOUT REVISITING AND REVISING WHAT YOU THINK YOU HAVE DECIDED.

IRRELEVANCE IS WHAT HAPPENS WHEN YOU SIMPLY STOP WHILE THE REST OF THE WORLD KEEPS MOVING.

Think about this.

Irrelevance doesn't just happen. Anything irrelevant in your ministry was probably relevant at one time. I doubt it became irrelevant in a day. It was gradual. Irrelevance is what happens when you simply stop while the rest of the world keeps moving. That's why you need to create a culture that actively pursues innovation and change. Collaboration connects leaders who have a holy dissatisfaction with the status quo, because they know too much is at stake if they simply try to maintain.

SO, IMPROV OR DIE.

If you don't innovate, you'll watch your potential influence in this world fade away.

That's one of the reasons the rest of this book, including this chapter, taps into a wider host of thinkers. Thinkers and leaders from inside and outside the Orange family have loaned me their expertise to help complete this collection of game-changing ideas.

Jon Williams
Writer, actor, and master at improvisation and calculus

Casey Graham
Entrepreneur, executive pastor, and church financial growth innovator

Kristen Ivy
Baylor cheerleader, seminary graduate, and long-term Small Group Leader

Elizabeth Hansen
Script writer, creative director, and advocate for Harry

Matt McKee
Family ministry director, social media coach, and app developer

These pages were heavily influenced by their contributions.

IT'S YOUR TURN: **COLLABORATE**

HOW CAN YOU INCORPORATE THE FIVE TEAM PRINCIPLES
FOR THE SAKE OF INNOVATION IN YOUR MINISTRY?

HERE ARE SOME IDEAS
ADD YOUR OWN

PERSONALIZE IT
FOR YOU

Grade yourself on the five team principles at the end of the chapter. Then ask someone who works with you if they agree.

STRATEGIZE IT
WITH YOUR TEAM

Plan a series of meetings over the next few months where each staff member puts something they are trying to improve on the table. Allow each staff member to give input.

ORANGIFY IT
FOR THE NEXT GENERATION

Invite members of the next generation into a strategy meeting. Ask them what they would change if they were in charge.

COLLABORATE TO DISCOVER
THE BEST IDEAS AND SOLUTIONS

WINE WILL BE CHEAPER THAN GAS

STAY SOBER AND GROW FINANCIALLY IN A TIPSY ECONOMY

7

WINE WILL BE CHEAPER THAN GAS.

THIS STATEMENT IS NOT ONLY RELEVANT TO THOSE WHO DRINK WINE. IT'S ALSO SIGNIFICANT FOR THE REST OF US WHO DROP CHANGE ON GOURMET COFFEE OR HEALTHY SMOOTHIES.

You don't have to be an economist to realize the economy has been taking us all on a roller coaster ride with more plunges than climbs. Here are some of the statements I've heard this year:

- Gas is so expensive, wherever you're going on vacation it might be cheaper to mail your car.

- Hot Wheels cars are trading higher than the Chevy Volt.

- Wall Street is now being called Walmart Street.

- The economy is so bad, my ATM gave me an IOU!

- Did you get your pre-declined credit card today?

- I can afford to buy my house, just not sell it.

THE ECONOMY HAS BEEN TAKING US ALL ON A ROLLER COASTER RIDE WITH MORE PLUNGES THAN CLIMBS.

Words like foreclosure, recession, and unemployment are the dialect of the day in our tipsy economy.

Who wouldn't like a time machine to hop back to the sunny financial climate prior to the 2008 crisis?

Craig A. Elwell, a specialist in macroeconomic policy, released a report to the U.S. Congress in December 2011. He speaks about the new reality,

"There is concern that this time the U.S. economy will either not return to its pre-recession growth path but perhaps remain permanently below it, or return to the pre-crisis path but at a slower than normal pace."[1]

I read recently in the *Washington Post* that "churches lost $1.2 billion in [the] recession."[2] As we travel the country working with church leaders, we consistently hear how this new reality has strained ministry.

In fact, a recent survey of nearly 1,100 churches by GivingRocket.com found only 14 percent of churches are exceeding budget.[3]

14%

Depressing, I know. But what if our current economic climate has a bright side? It's interesting that according to many experts, hard times actually have the potential to drive innovation. "Learning to do more with less is a design philosophy that is newly relevant, creatively-rich, and economically viable. Constraints stretch flabby design muscles; the results are often surprisingly buff."[4]

GAME

A NEW ECONOMIC REALITY IS CREATING AN OPPORTUNITY TO INNOVATE HEALTHIER FINANCIAL STRATEGIES.

CHANGER

HERE'S A CONFESSION:

EVERYONE WHO KNOWS ME IS VERY AWARE THAT FINANCIAL MANAGEMENT IS NOT MY NUMBER ONE STRENGTH.

(It's not number two or three either.)

So, for the past few months I have spent some time with people smarter than me.

Casey Graham is one of those.

Casey is the founder of Giving Rocket.

His team collaborates and innovates strategies to help churches win financially. That's why I interviewed him about churches and the economy. During our conversations, I found myself wishing every church leader could listen. He reinforced the idea that the new economy is a game-changer. The present financial situation is transforming the way churches need to think about stewardship.

CONSIDER THE FOLLOWING IDEAS:

- The way people view money has changed significantly.

- You can't control *the* economy, but you can control *your* economy.

- The stock market is out of your control, but what happens in your budget planning meeting isn't.

- Fear-mongering by the media is out of your control, but the way you talk about money isn't.

We're not going to single-handedly rein in the economy.

It just won't happen.

But there are things we *can* control to make a vital difference in fully funding our churches.

Have you ever stopped to think that the best time to cast a new vision for the financial growth of your church could be when the economy is struggling? Maybe now is actually the best time to rally your staff around some new rules relating to money.

Here are just a few of the principles Casey and his team are helping churches understand.

1

Think Systems, Not Silver Bullets

When things get tight, many churches reach for a silver bullet:

- Spending freezes
- Poorly-designed fundraisers
- And don't forget those last-minute sermons on generosity... .

    But silver-bullet thinking won't change culture. Instead of looking for quick solutions, you need a well-coordinated plan of attack for your entire financial system.

Your church probably has a spending system or a spending plan,

but do you have a funding system?

Your church might have a team or committee responsible for financial oversight, but is there a team of people who focus on increasing operational revenue?

What if the ministry team leaders met and said, "How will we increase regular giving over the next twelve months?"

Imagine the synergy from aligning ministry leaders around the idea of fully funding ALL ministries. This isn't a job for the executive pastor, senior pastor, bookkeeper or finance team— it's a job for every team member who wants to see ministry thrive.

2

Own the Outcome

The GivingRocket.com Church Giving Survey shows 42 percent of churches say that increasing operational giving is on "no one's job description."[5]

Oops.

- How does your ministry staff get paid?

- How do you pay for your children's ministry environments?
- What allows you to fix things when they break?
- What allows you to accomplish your vision?

Money.

We can try to over-spiritualize this issue but at the end of the day it takes money to do ministry. And in a lot of churches, NO ONE is responsible for the ONE thing that can cripple the ministry faster than anything else.

If you want to create your own economy in your church, someone has to own the responsibility of increasing church giving so we can have more money for ministry.

Who is going to own this major issue in your church?

We suggest you take a **team approach** and involve your key players in owning this issue, because it affects every ministry and every person in your church.

After all, your ministry cannot thrive unless you have the financial resources to invest in your priorities.

Fund Their Dreams, Not Just Yours

"Want something **for** your people, not just **from** your people."

This statement by Andy Stanley inspired Pastor Carey Nieuwhof of Connexus Community Church in Barrie, Ontario, Canada, to do something different in 2011.

The church had been growing rapidly, but income wasn't keeping up with the growth. Margin was non-existent, and they were a few months from a deficit.

So, Connexus launched an initiative called *Thrive* to help people "live with margin so they can live on mission."

This was about wanting something for THEM—the people—not just the church.

Carey cast a vision that he wanted every family to be able to take a debt-free vacation over the next year.

The church also asked people to jump onboard and live a life on mission by giving to the vision of their church as well.

Twelve months later, more people in the congregation are thriving financially ... and Connexus Community Church exceeded budget by 23 percent.

For far too long, churches have just asked for 10 percent, but never bothered to help people with the other 90 percent.

When is the last time your leadership team spent time strategizing on how to help the people in your church go on a family vacation and pay for it with cash?

When is the last time you thought about investing in personal financial help for the people in your church?

The people in your church can't change THE economy, but they can change THEIR economy in their own homes.

THE CHURCH GIVING SURVEY CONFIRMS THIS TRUTH:

OFFERING PERSONAL FINANCIAL HELP FOR THE PEOPLE IN THE CHURCH IS THE THIRD HIGHEST INFLUENCER FOR CHURCHES EXCEEDING BUDGET.

So, are you wondering what the #1 and #2 influencers are?

1
Automated giving

2
Effective online giving sites[6]

Just in case that seems extreme, think about it for a minute.

Is giving an act of worship? Does giving have anything to do with spiritual growth?

Then shouldn't leaders make it as easy as possible for people to give?

These past few years, money has been a complicated issue for a lot of churches. Christian leaders are recognizing they have an increasing responsibility in an economy where people are hurting financially. This issue of financial stewardship is just as spiritual as prayer or Bible study.

Some might argue that, for some individuals, it's more important. If a messy Gospel requires you to make sacrifices for the sake of helping others know Christ, chances are that's going to cost you some change—not just changes, but literal cash. Money is linked to the mission of the church; it was important in the New Testament, and it still is today. You are called to lead people to restore and redeem a broken world.

Yes, only God's Spirit and the power of His Gospel can forgive and heal the heart, but more than likely, it's going to cost some money to fix everything else. Do you really think it's possible to lead people into a growing relationship with Jesus Christ, without getting involved with the financial side of their lives?

THERE'S A REASON **JESUS ...**

- told a rich young ruler he should give away everything he had and follow Jesus.
- illustrated sacrifice with a widow who gave away the little that she had.
- taught that your heart would ultimately follow your treasure.

There is a link between faith and money. So, if churches plan to lead a generation into a deeper faith, they will have to be a model in what they say and do regarding money. In a tipsy economy, it's actually a spiritual issue for the church to stay financially sober.

So, think systems instead of silver bullets:
- take responsibility for the outcome
- help people fund their dreams
- lead a generation to trust God with their money.

IT'S YOUR TURN: # COLLABORATE

WHAT ARE THREE THINGS YOU WOULD LIKE TO SEE CHANGE IN YOUR OVERALL FINANCIAL SITUATION THIS NEXT YEAR?

HERE ARE SOME IDEAS ADD YOUR OWN

PERSONALIZE IT
FOR YOU

STRATEGIZE IT
WITH YOUR TEAM

ORANGIFY IT
FOR THE NEXT GENERATION

Choose to manage your personal economy by creating a monthly spending plan and living on less than you make.

Discuss one of the Giving Rocket principles and what it would look like to implement it in your church.

Consider teaching an age-appropriate financial series for families that help children and students learn to manage money.

STAY SOBER AND GROW FINANCIALLY IN A TIPSY ECONOMY

THE CLOUD IS HERE

LEARN TO NAVIGATE IN A HYPER-CONNECTED WORLD

8

For almost 30 YEARS we tweaked our home electronics.

We upgraded ...
- our AM radios to FM stereo
- our TVs to color
- our eight tracks to cassettes
- and our phones to cordless

Then, in the early 1980s, a fundamental shift happened.

Personal computers showed up and transformed the way we lived at home.

When I think about how technology has changed in my dad's lifetime, it's quite staggering.

Dad was born in **1937 during the Depression** on a cotton farm in east Georgia.

He was eight years old when **World War II** ended and their house got electricity.

He was 15 years old when **Eisenhower became President**, and they got a telephone.

Around that same time **radio** and then **television** became standard items for most households.

My dad's job was evaluating confidential data and military equipment specs for the government. I'm pretty sure he actually built a computer before Steve Jobs. So, he was skeptical when I spent a few thousand dollars on a square beige box called a MacPlus in 1986. I still remember some of his comments.

"THIS IS A FAD. I'M NOT SURE IT'S GOING TO LAST."
"GET THE 20 MEG HARD DRIVE, IT'S ALL YOU'LL EVER NEED."
"ONE DAY I'LL GET YOU A REAL COMPUTER."

Then a decade later ...
Cellular phones gave us mobility
and the Internet opened a bigger
window to the world than we
had ever imagined.

Another decade passed and ...
Digital formatting changed the
way we listened to music,
watched video,
and used cameras.

Then in 2004 ...
Facebook turned the globe into
a social gathering.

And shortly afterwards ...
Smart phones put the world
in our hands to carry with us
everywhere we go.

HERE'S HOW I RECAP
THE PAST CENTURY:

- Telephones connected my home
  to your home.
- Then radio and television
  connected my home to
  entertainment and news.
- Then personal computers
  connected my home to my work.
- Then mobile phones connected
  me to you.
- Then the Internet connected me
  to information.
- Then digital formatting
  connected me to more
  entertainment.
- Then Facebook connected all of
  us to each other.

NOW A SMART DEVICE
CONNECTS ALL OF US
TO EACH OTHER,
EVERYTHING,
EVERYWHERE,
ALL THE TIME.

This is a hyper-connected world.
How we connect and communicate
has been redefined forever.

For the first time in history, the social aspect of our lives is with us twenty-four-seven. Hundreds of people including your co-workers, your friends, your family, even strangers are with you

IN THE BATHROOM,
IN THE CAR,
IN THE OFFICE,
IN THE KITCHEN,
IN THE STORE,
IN THE CLASSROOM.

If Starbucks gave culture a third place to be social between home and work, as we explain in the next chapter, smart devices recreated the entire world as a virtual third place.

It's now everywhere.
You are always in it.
The cloud is here.

People no longer live online; online now lives with people.

This is a big game-changer because it affects everything and everyone. It's even a game-changer that influences other game-changers. Everything we have written about in this book is directly or indirectly affected by the virtual reality of what the cloud symbolizes. I'm not even sure I could have written this book without the cloud.

It's not just that social media has changed the *way* we can connect, but it is redefining the nature of *how* we connect. The transformation within culture is much deeper than simply the notion that we have more access. Technology changes in the past may have improved how we access and use information. But social media has created a new set of rules that are transforming the language and psychology of relationships.

At its core, social media is escalating for one reason.

 IT'S SOCIAL.

If you forget that, you will miss the essence of how it works.

The need and desire for people to connect with people is timeless.

EVERYTHING WE HAVE WRITTEN ABOUT IN THIS BOOK IS DIRECTLY OR INDIRECTLY AFFECTED BY THE VIRTUAL REALITY OF WHAT THE CLOUD SYMBOLIZES.

The implications of the cloud are almost too endless to discuss. But savvy leaders wrestle with understanding it because they know intuitively it affects how they connect and communicate with this generation. It's simply too huge to ignore.

 THE CLOUD IS HERE and it suggests a new set of priorities for the average leader. You can no longer assume that conventional ways to communicate and nurture relationships work. People expect you to speak their language, and social media is the new universal language. Effective leaders have to learn how to connect with people in the way those individuals connect. And more people are choosing to connect through some type of social media.

CONSIDER THE FACTS:
96 percent of Millennials are on a social network.[1]

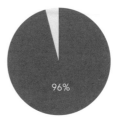

81 percent of children under the age of two already have a "digital profile."[2]

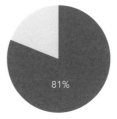

Generations X, Y and Z consider email old-fashioned.[3]

It's simple.

Leaders who want to connect with the next generation will have to make understanding social media a priority. It's becoming increasingly important for leaders who care about people to jump in and become social media competent. A leading branding company suggests that leaders who use social media raise their organization's visibility, create confidence among their staff, and build trust among the people they serve.[4]

So, it may be time to get serious about your social media skills. The cloud is where we live now, and I see three important categories of people emerging:

- Those who are social media TOURISTS
- Those who are social media CITIZENS
- Those who are social media NATIVES

Did you notice who is not on the list? I don't really have a category for those who don't use social media. I'm sure they exist. I just don't know them. My dad is 75, and even he seems to be moving toward citizenship. Those who are off-the-grid have to be minimal in number.

How do I know?

Well considering there are "more people using smart phones than there are people using toothbrushes," [5] it seems obvious the majority are living in the cloud.

That said, I have to admit I am barely a social media citizen who will never make it to native status. I know my

strengths. Social media is not one. That doesn't mean I shouldn't learn how to live effectively in the cloud. Avoiding the cloud is not an option if I want to connect better with those who are important to me.

That's why you should strive to become a social media citizen.

One of the most important things a leader can do is to move beyond the tourist level. A tourist plays in the social media world and knows just enough to get around. It's not wrong to be a tourist, but you can usually spot them. And the problem is, natives tend to avoid tourists who don't care enough to learn their language or understand their culture.

So, if you want to earn respect from social media natives and build a relationship with this generation, you have to pursue learning how social media works. Our children are growing up as natives who feel like they belong in the cloud. They are becoming a tribe who will move naturally within this virtual world. But the point is, if you are called to lead in this culture, you need to get in social media school. As a next generation leader, you should strive to become a good social media citizen. If you hope to connect, communicate, or have influence with this tribe you will have to learn to speak their language.

Honestly, it's tricky for me.
The cloud is moving so fast.
As soon as I think I understand
The rules change again.

FOR EXAMPLE:

Phone calls now can be
considered intrusive.

Texts are not considered
interruptions.

When you text, you are expected to
respond promptly.

Never reply to the full group in a
group text message.

If you hope to be quoted, it needs to
be 140 characters or less.

Twitter has eliminated this question in
culture: "What did you do today?"

You are responsible to know what
happened to someone today,
if they posted it.

Don't email a complaint. Post it on
your blog.

Some of your closest friends are no
longer in your zip code.

Words like Facebook, friend, and
message are now verbs.

But the most important rule of all is to
remember that social media is social.

PAUSE FOR A
MOMENT.

THINK ABOUT
THIS POTENTIAL.
I NO LONGER HAVE TO
BE PHYSICALLY PRESENT,
TO MAKE A MEANINGFUL
CONNECTION.

AND DON'T TRY TO
CONVINCE ME THAT
IT'S SUPERFICIAL OR
ARTIFICIAL.

My experience has been just the
opposite. Be careful that you don't
carelessly discount the cloud's
potential to connect people in a
meaningful way. That's what tourists
do, because they don't really
understand the essence of the culture.
The fact that everyone is hyper-
connected means ...

YOU CAN CONNECT WITH PEOPLE YOU KNEW.

In the past few years I have reconnected with people I have not had contact with for decades.

Scott was my best friend in elementary through high school. Until last year, our most recent connection was in the 1980s.

So now I know ...
- whenever he gets to see his son who is in the military
- whenever there's news about his family
- whenever he finds a 70s vintage item on eBay

YOU CAN CONNECT WITH PEOPLE WHO NEED TO CONNECT.

Last year, I had some important virtual conversations that included ...

- A young pastor's wife whose husband unexpectedly committed suicide
- A seminary student questioning a vocation decision
- A teenager struggling in a relationship with his parents
- A Christian leader going through a divorce
- A parent with a Down Syndrome child

WHEN YOU CAN'T BE PHYSICALLY PRESENT, YOU CAN STILL CULTIVATE MEANINGFUL FRIENDSHIPS.

WHEN YOU CAN'T BE PHYSICALLY PRESENT, YOU CAN STILL HAVE CRITICAL CONVERSATIONS.

YOU CAN CONNECT WITH PEOPLE CREATIVELY.

YOU CAN CONNECT WITH PEOPLE IN DEEPER WAYS.

Now you can give people space to think through something before they show up for a face-to-face meeting. Small group leaders are learning to use it to prompt their group for discussions before they show up. As a parent, I have realized it's a creative way to connect with my own kids about certain issues instead of calling them. It can actually be a non-threatening way to begin a difficult conversation with people who tend to shut down during confrontation.

I know some think conversations in the cloud are shallow.

I could argue the exact same thing about conversations you have in person.

All I know is that a host of people in my world seem to express themselves more clearly and deeply when they message or blog.

WHEN YOU AREN'T PHYSICALLY PRESENT, YOU CAN MAKE BETTER CONNECTIONS THAN YOU WOULD IN PERSON.

WHEN YOU DON'T WANT TO BE PHYSICALLY PRESENT, YOU CAN STILL EXPRESS YOURSELF— MAYBE EVEN BETTER.

THAT'S WHY YOU SHOULD STRIVE TO BECOME A SOCIAL MEDIA CITIZEN.

Today, more than ever before, churches have incredible potential to engage people where they are—in the cloud.

ARE YOU STARTING TO GET THE VISION?
HERE ARE SOME FAST TIPS IF YOU'RE READY TO BE SERIOUS ABOUT BECOMING A SOCIAL MEDIA CITIZEN:

Prioritize it on the calendar.

Right now. Block out some hours this week. Just to learn and practice. Earn your citizenship.

Google it.

The best information about living in the cloud is actually in the cloud. Start here: www.socialmediatoday.com

Get a personal technical coach.

Find a native who will hang out with you and teach you. There's probably one in your student ministry.

Create a top 10 list.

Bookmark the top experts on social media. You might bookmark the best reviews on tools and apps too.

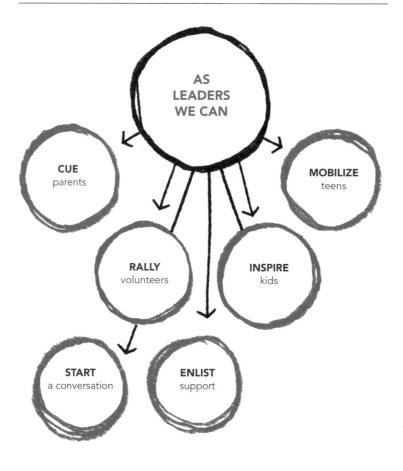

But you can only make a fraction of those connections if you have to do it in person.

WHEN YOU VIRTUALLY CONNECT ...
You can connect with people in ways you can't if you are physically present.
You can solve complicated problems for multiple people at the same time.
You can listen and understand more about people's concerns and issues.
You can learn more about Harry.

Here's something else to consider.

Today, more than ever before, churches have incredible potential to engage people where they are—in the cloud. After all, finding information about God is one of the top reasons people use the Internet.[6] Nine million more people participate in Christian media than go to Christian churches.[7]

OUR CALLING IS TO

love people

help people

influence people with the Gospel.

When Jesus told His followers to "go and make disciples of all nations,"8 they were limited by their own two feet in reaching the world. Now, we literally have the world at our fingertips.

SO, MAYBE WE SHOULD BECOME MISSIONARIES IN THE CLOUD.

That means we need to do what good missionaries do.

- STUDY **THE CULTURE**
- LEARN **THE LANGUAGE**
- CONNECT **WITH PEOPLE**

Learn to live in the world of social media.

To reach 50 million users, it took radio 38 years it took television 13 years and it took the Internet four years. Facebook added 200 million users in less than a year. Mobile apps hit one billion users in nine months. [8]

What we could never do when we were trying to be physically present, is now possible to do by being virtually present.

It actually may be more important to connect with this generation virtually than it is physically.

Okay, maybe not. But you'll need to read the next chapter to decide.

IT'S YOUR TURN: COLLABORATE

WHAT ARE SOME KEY WAYS SOCIAL MEDIA CAN HELP
YOUR CHURCH CONNECT WITH YOUR COMMUNITY AND
CONGREGATION?

HERE ARE SOME IDEAS
ADD YOUR OWN

PERSONALIZE IT
FOR YOU

Schedule a regular time to use a new (to you) social media tool to listen to and connect. (Here are a few you might try: Facebook, Twitter, Google Reader, Pinterest, RSS feeds or WordPress, Tumblr, Instagram, YouTube, Vimeo.)

STRATEGIZE IT
WITH YOUR TEAM

Consider having someone who is advanced in social media skills train your staff on a consistent basis. (They may already be on your staff, so give them a few minutes each month.)

ORANGIFY IT
FOR THE NEXT GENERATION

Invite students who are natives in this area to social media brainstorming sessions, and allow them to work on special media assignments with your staff.

NAVIGATE STRATEGICALLY
IN A HYPER-CONNECTED WORLD

THIRD PLACE STILL WINS

MAKE IT EASY FOR SOMEONE TO EXPERIENCE COMMUNITY

9

So, do you think it's more important in this culture to be virtually present, or physically present?

WALK INTO ANY STARBUCKS AND WHAT DO YOU SEE?

- High school study groups
- Business meetings
- Moms
- Musicians
- Maybe even a bald guy working on a book about zombies

Starbucks is more than a place to purchase coffee.

**It's a place to connect.
It's personal and it's social.
It's where people want to be.**

Sociologist Ray Oldenburg developed the concept of "the third place" in his book, *The Great Good Place.* The third place is different from home (the first place) or work (the second place.) It's a third place where people connect socially, find an entry point, meet old friends and make some new ones.

He wrote the book in 1989, coincidentally the same year Starbucks started its expansion from a few dozen stores to more than **16,000** coffeehouses around the world.

In his book *Onward*, Howard Shultz writes, "If home is the primary or 'first' place where a person connects with others, and if work is a person's 'second place,' then a public space such as a coffeehouse—such as Starbucks—is what I have always referred to as the 'third place.'"[1]

Since its beginning, Starbucks has placed a priority on becoming third place in the hearts and minds of its customers. That vision drives everything from barista training to music playlists and furniture arrangement.

And it's working.

In the midst of economic recession, Starbucks grossed $7.35 billion this past year selling a "luxury" commodity. Maybe it's because they are an incredibly savvy business. Maybe it's because we're all caffeine-addicts. Or maybe it's because third place still wins.

Third place doesn't just win when it comes to adults and their coffee.

Third place is the reason
- little girls gather inside American Girl Boutiques
- little boys spend Saturdays at the ballpark
- teenagers form clubs dedicated to their love of Harry

EVERYONE WANTS

 A group
A circle
A tribe

These relationships shape who we are and how we interpret the world around us.

Research suggests that our ability to connect authentically directly affects our emotional and spiritual well-being. The path to finding healthy autonomy and identity is paved with a sense of belonging.

IT'S IRONIC:

WE NEED OTHERS IN OUR LIVES TO HELP US BECOME INDEPENDENT.

So now let's get back to that mass rush to connect through the cloud. Social media provides quick access to relationships. And there's no denying the significant effect of social media on the next generation.

As we have already implied, it's become the virtual third place.

THERE'S NO DENYING THE SIGNIFICANT EFFECT OF SOCIAL MEDIA ON THE NEXT GENERATION.

HERE ARE SOME MORE SOCIAL MEDIA STATS FOR YOU TO TWEET:

From 2005-2010, the percent of 8- to 18-year-olds who own a cell phone rose from 39 percent to 66 percent, and from 18 percent to 76 percent for iPods and other MP3 players.[2]

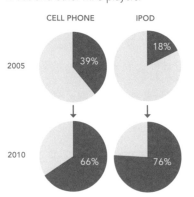

CELL PHONE IPOD

2005

2010

Teenagers are waiting longer to get their driver's licenses because they no longer feel the need to be in the same place as their friends in order to be with their friends. In fact, Gartner Research cited in the Lempert Report that nearly half (46 percent) of 18- to 24-year-olds would pick Internet access over having their own car.[4]

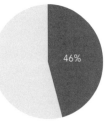

PERCENTAGE OF 18-24 YR OLDS THAT WOULD PICK INTERNET OVER HAVING THEIR OWN CAR

In 2011, 64 percent of 12- to 13-year-olds, and 88 percent of 14- to 17-year-olds, reported using social media. From 2009 to 2011 the percentage of teens on Twitter has doubled.[3]

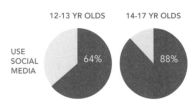

12-13 YR OLDS   14-17 YR OLDS

USE SOCIAL MEDIA

From a study of seven thousand 16- to 30-year-olds across the UK, US, Spain, China, Brazil, India and Mexico: 53 percent of those between the ages of 16 and 22 would give up their sense of smell rather than sacrifice their social networks.[5]

This generation is more connected than any generation that's come before. And this generation is redefining what it means to connect.

But here's the question. **Does embracing the world of media-driven connectedness make in-the-same-room, face-to-face community more or less important?**

When you connect virtually, you—
- Have more control over your public image
- Can speak without having to listen
- Don't feel the immediate implications of your words

When you are physically present, you—
- See others through multiple impressions
- Connect through physical realities
- Experience un-edited emotions

In the virtual third place, you can connect:
- conveniently
- anytime
- anywhere

In a physical third place, you connect:
- sacrificially
- in a specific place
- at a specific time

GAME

SOCIAL MEDIA IS INCREASING THE VALUE OF BEING PHYSICALLY PRESENT IN ORDER TO CONNECT.

CHANGER

Why does the growth of social media actually elevate the importance of a physical third place?

Because being in the cloud with someone doesn't send the same message as being in the same room with them.

Social media can potentially highlight the contrast between being connected virtually and being together physically.

I already told you about the advantages of living in the cloud. So, don't backtrack on me. The cloud is still important. It allows you to connect even when you can't be physically present.

It permits you to be wherever you need or want to be while you keep the conversation going.

But when you connect through the cloud, you're always somewhere else.

Maybe that's why social media can make someone feel connected to you, but a physical third place will make someone feel important to you in a more significant way.

It's why—

- Couples who meet online decide on a place to go for their first date.
- Friends buy airline tickets and travel across the country to attend a wedding.
- Parents and grandparents sit through incredibly long graduation ceremonies.
- People will change their plans to show up at the wake of a family friend.

When we take the time to show up and be physically present, it makes a statement. It communicates

- Value
- Significance
- Love

That's why the Christian community has a unique opportunity, now more than ever before. In a world of online relationships, this generation needs adults who will show up and be present in their lives. They need spiritual leaders who will believe in them and give them a sense of belonging and worth.

THEY NEED A PHYSICAL THIRD PLACE.

Christian community does not exist simply for the sake of community. Christian community exists as a means for building authentic faith.

When I look at studies about young adults who are walking away from church, it seems that nothing is more significant to passing on a spiritual legacy than connecting children and teenagers with adults in genuine, authentic community.

When a kid connects to other adults in a community of faith:
- They establish a sense of belonging.
- They feel significant to God's story.
- They experience God's grace.

"Our kids don't yet know themselves, yet they desperately want to be known."[7]

– Chap Clark

"More than any single program or event, adults making the effort to get to know the kids was far more likely to make the kids feel like a significant part of their church."[8]

– Kara Powell

"Kids experience Jesus Christ when adults in the church give them grace, time, and genuine love with no hidden agenda."[9]

– John and Nancy Ortenberg

Maybe it's time for the church to remember the words of Paul to the church in Thessalonica:

We loved you so much, we were delighted to share with you not only the Gospel of God but our lives as well.[10]

If the church is going to win the hearts of the next generation, it must fight to connect every child with an adult who is eager to care, love, and share—not just the Gospel—but their life as well.

The church needs to take the value of third place seriously.

How?

There will be a lot of creative answers over the next several years. But here are three examples of what I think it can look like for churches that want to be third place.

CHRISTIAN COMMUNITY DOES NOT EXIST SIMPLY FOR THE SAKE OF COMMUNITY. CHRISTIAN COMMUNITY EXISTS AS A MEANS FOR BUILDING AUTHENTIC FAITH.

1

Third place wins when it reminds us to connect more adults to kids, not more adults to programs.

What if you could connect five adults to every one kid?
There's nothing magical about the number five—
Unless you're a conspiracy theorist.

A Lifeway study of students after graduation found, "More of those who stayed in church☐by a margin of 46 percent to 28 percent☐said five or more adults at church had invested time with them personally and spiritually."[11]

In *Parenting Beyond Your Capacity*, Carey Nieuwhof shares the significance of creating a "mentoring year" in which he and his son identified five men in their relational circle, who could intentionally spend one day imparting spiritual and practical truth at a critical time in his son's life.[12]

In *Sticky Faith*, Chap Clark argues that we need to reverse the "1:5 ratio of adults to kids for their Sunday school class or small groups." He asks the question, "What if we said we want a 5:1 adult-to-kid ratio—five adults caring for each kid?"[13]

I'm not suggesting that every kid who grows up in your ministry needs five small group leaders. I'm not even suggesting that the church is responsible for finding all of the adults who will invest in the life of a child. I'm suggesting that in order to think third place, the church should think strategically about relationships that happen over time, in multiple environments, to physically connect adults to the next generation.

Think about it this way:
The cloud will connect this generation to hundreds of people who can

- Provide advice
- Interpret daily events
- Live as public examples

But the church has a unique opportunity to connect kids with Christian adults who will value them enough to be physically present in order to—

- Help them interpret life.
- Support them in times of tragedy.
- Carry them through life transitions.

Third place wins when it focuses on the quality of community, not the quantity of attendance.

"We had 200 students sign up for Disciple Now."

"450 kids attended our VBS last summer."

"Sunday attendance has grown every week this past quarter."

Sound familiar?

It should. And statements like these should excite you. We instinctively celebrate growing numbers because we want to have a big influence in the next generation. But what if the biggest influence you could have really happens by doing something small?

This generation craves connection more than the generations before them.[14]

But they are not coming to church so they can find *more* connections. They are coming because they want a *better* connection.

They are yearning for a sense of community that isn't found anywhere else in culture.

Why don't you create the kind of authentic third place that this generation needs? Organize small groups around adults who will be physically present in the lives of a few in order to encourage authentic faith.

In the book *Lead Small*, we explain a few big ideas. The next generation needs leaders who will—

- **Be present** to *connect* their faith to a community.
- **Create a safe place** to *clarify* their faith as they grow.
- **Partner with parents** to *nurture* everyday faith.
- **Make it personal** to *inspire* their faith by example.
- **Move them out** to *engage* their faith in a bigger story.[15]

As you evaluate your ministries, it might be helpful to ask yourself this question:

Are they coming to an event or are they connecting with a leader?

3

Third place wins when it provides meaningful experiences—not just great information.

Take a minute and Google the following phrases

CHRISTIAN GOSPEL
GREAT COMMANDMENT
SERMON ON THE MOUNT

I don't know everything you will discover, but I'm willing to bet that in a matter of seconds, you will find a whole LOT of information.

This generation isn't just connected to more virtual relationships, they are connected to more information as well.

But that information is

UNEDITED
UNVERIFIED
NOT PRIORITIZED

Here's the point.

When you make it a priority to be physically present you can create an experience that *connects the dots*. A quick Google search could probably give an individual the critical

information for faith. But if they do the searching alone, they will probably never personalize it for themselves.

When we establish a physical third place, we not only pass on essential information, we will do it in a way that is personal and transformational.

If we are in the business of creating a physical third place, we have to stop thinking about putting children and teenagers in rows in order to teach them information.

We need to start thinking about putting every child and every teenager in a circle where they can

PROCESS DOUBT
ASK HARD QUESTIONS
WRESTLE WITH COMPLICATED IDEAS

If kids are not allowed to have experiences where they process their doubts, they may never own their own faith.

When you make it a priority to be physically present you can create the kind of experience that *engages them in a mission*.

If we are in the business of creating a generation with a faith that lasts, we have to stop thinking only about what the church can DO for kids and start asking how can we invite them to BE the church.

As much as information matters, experience matters more.

Remember: in chapter one we said,

"This generation doesn't need a new and improved version of Sunday school. They need to engage in a passionate adventure outside the walls of a church building."

When you create a third place you connect them to leaders who will be with them while they experience the mission of a messy Gospel.

In his research at Baylor, Michael Sherr concludes, "Young people need to work in authentic service that meets real human needs and have a chance to reflect on these experiences with adults in order to experience a deepening faith."[16]

 Did you catch that?

When a kid serves *with* adults, their service is more impactful. Missions and service can't be done virtually. It takes physical presence. And when service is intergenerational, it creates a powerful third place experience that ignites the faith of the next generation.

So, I guess third place actually wins. You may be surprised to hear me say this, but I think it wins over the cloud.

The cloud is the most revolutionary idea of our time. It has the potential to significantly enhance what can happen when we are present with each other. But it doesn't replace physical presence.

WHEN YOU MAKE IT A PRIORITY TO BE PHYSICALLY PRESENT YOU CAN CREATE AN EXPERIENCE THAT CONNECTS THE DOTS.

Apple, the company that popularized the phrase "the cloud," still has physical stores.

Starbucks, the company that champions the third place, didn't lose business when social media was interjected.

In fact, some people say Starbucks is in the business of selling an affordable luxury—coffee. But Howard Schultz says that in reality, they are marketing an affordable necessity—personal connection. "We are all hungry for community."[17]

 Don't miss this.

Smart leaders will discover ways social media can help third place win.

And effective leaders will remember Third place will always win.

IF WE ARE IN THE BUSINESS OF CREATING A GENERATION WITH A FAITH THAT LASTS, WE HAVE TO STOP THINKING ONLY ABOUT WHAT THE CHURCH CAN DO FOR KIDS AND START ASKING HOW CAN WE INVITE THEM TO BE THE CHURCH.

IT'S YOUR TURN: # COLLABORATE

WHAT CAN YOUR CHURCH DO TO MOTIVATE ADULTS TO SHOW UP PREDICTABLY IN THE LIVES OF CHILDREN AND TEENAGERS?

HERE ARE SOME IDEAS
ADD YOUR OWN

PERSONALIZE IT
FOR YOU

STRATEGIZE IT
WITH YOUR TEAM

ORANGIFY IT
FOR THE NEXT
GENERATION

Identify the people who embody a third place for you and commit to spending time together on a regular basis.

Organize your ministries to move people into small groups. Or if you already have small groups, plan times for those groups to engage in ministry together.

Run a fifth year experiment. Challenge small group leaders who have groups of seniors, to take one year to stay connected to their group as they transition into college or their next life stage.

MAKE IT EASY FOR SOMEONE TO EXPERIENCE COMMUNITY

EVERY-BODY KNOWS HARRY

TELL STORIES IN A WAY THAT CAPTIVATES THE IMAGINATION

10

Why has this generation been so intrigued by the tale of Harry Potter? Whether you are a fan or not, you have to admit that Harry has become a cultural icon.

On July 21, 2007,

the final volume, *Harry Potter and the Deathly Hallows*, became the fastest-selling book in history, with more than 11 million copies sold during the first 24 hours in three markets.[1]

We all know the story of a certain boy, an unusual boy, marked for a specific destiny from his birth. As he discovered his true identity and embraced his purpose, he grew in wisdom and strength. His closest friends followed him everywhere, facing grave opposition, but even they could not always understand what he understood. And even they could not follow him into the very final battle against an evil enemy, where he entered into death itself ... and defeated it.

It's interesting that this generation is drawn toward the power of story, especially any story that reflects the overarching themes of Scripture.

I honestly wonder what God thinks about Harry.

That's probably a risky thought to confess. But I'm curious. I'm pretty sure God's not surprised when He sees His ancient narrative echoed through the writing of an author He's created in His image. I'm not trying to make judgments about Harry, just observations about the fact that he inspires so many.

Does the story sound familiar? It should.

Because everybody knows Harry.

I'm not sure Harry's any different than ...
Luke Skywalker in *Star Wars*
Frodo in *Lord of the Rings*
Woody in *Toy Story*

Maybe these stories show up every once in a while to remind us ...
of the struggle between good and evil
of the existence of a supernatural and miraculous power
of the potential to be personally restored and transformed

Have you ever wondered why certain themes are repeated?
Have you ever wondered where the idea of story originated?

Think about it:
God crafted an original script that would continue to fascinate humans.
Then He fashioned the human brain so it would connect to story.
I'm not sure which He did first, but either way it's an amazing strategy.

Experts have analyzed, theorized, and evangelized about the power of story.
Everyone seems to agree. It's as if our minds are hardwired to engage information as it fits together in the context of a narrative.

One specialist puts it this way:

In the last 15 years we have developed the brain imaging technologies that help us shed light on what it means to 'get lost' in a good story. Studies are suggesting that, when reading, listening or watching a good story, we activate brain regions used to process the experience as if it were our own. In other words, we are wired for stories.[2]

STORYTELLING IS BEING REVIVED.

Maybe that's the reason *everybody knows Harry.*

Harry is evidence that a well-crafted story and compelling characters have the potential to stimulate our gray matter. Storytelling is being revived.

In *A Whole New Mind*, Daniel Pink asserts that society has moved beyond the Information Age and into the Conceptual Age in which we are *"creators and empathizers," "pattern recognizers,"* and *"meaning makers."* Story is an important tool in this age because it enables us to *"encapsulate, contextualize and emotionalize."*[3]

In a world where we are constantly inundated by information, people have a renewed hunger for better stories, and it's changing the way leaders communicate. The power of story is being leveraged to

- **sell products during the Super Bowl**
- **create environments for video games**
- **explain business principles**
- **run political campaigns**
- **educate children in a classroom**

IT'S AS IF OUR MINDS ARE HARDWIRED TO ENGAGE INFORMATION AS IT FITS TOGETHER IN THE CONTEXT OF A NARRATIVE.

If you hire a consultant to help you in whatever you do, at some point they will probably ask you,

"What is the story you are trying to tell?"

Why? Because they understand your customers connect with stories. They also know that in the current flood of content your clients receive, only the most compelling stories rise to the top.

LEADERS ARE REDISCOVERING THE POWER OF STORY TO ENGAGE A CULTURE THAT IS OVER-SATURATED WITH INFORMATION.

In pre-Internet generations, information was more scarce. Those who succeeded were the ones who could gather it the fastest. The company with the best data and the library with the most books won.

But today, the rules have changed. Collecting information is no longer the goal. Now the greater need is to connect information, to sort ideas, to filter concepts and give content a better context. Those who win today are not as focused on collecting information as they are on connecting information.

THAT'S WHY STORIES ARE SO IMPORTANT AND SO RELEVANT TO THIS CULTURE.

I work with a team of creative editors, writers, and producers who eat, drink, and breathe the elements of story. They are the most passionate leaders I know when it comes to shaping a timeless story to influence the faith of kids, teenagers and families. We have learned a lot together over the past decade about developing environments, narratives, and characters that connect the dots for this generation.

COLLECTIVELY WE COULD WRITE VOLUMES ON WHAT WE HAVE
DISCOVERED ABOUT THE POWER OF STORY. IT WOULD INCLUDE
CHAPTERS ON ...

- **moral dilemmas**
- **smart dialogue**
- **character objectives**
- **cast design**

- **scene structure**
- **transformational characters**
- **comedy**
- **plot points**
- **and more**

**BUT IN THE END, A GOOD STORY
USUALLY COMES DOWN TO A
FEW THINGS.**

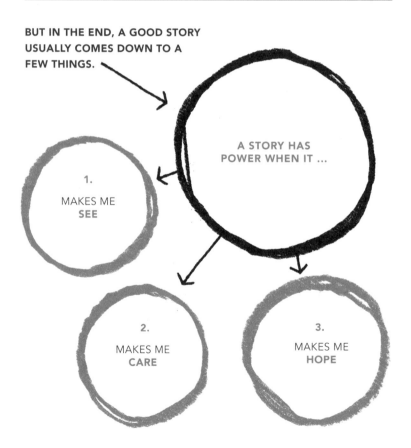

A STORY HAS
POWER WHEN IT ...

1.

MAKES ME
SEE

2.

MAKES ME
CARE

3.

MAKES ME
HOPE

1. Make me see.

Turn on the light.

Stories are multi faceted. They have a way of grouping and interpreting information. It's one reason high school students don't just study history. They read
The Crucible
Huckleberry Finn
Things Fall Apart
The Diary of Anne Frank

Story has the ability to help us see, and to give us deeper understanding. The most complicated principles in life have to be illustrated by life. Which is why I'm intrigued by the genius of the talented team at Pixar. Listen to what they say about story ...

We all love stories. We're born for them. Stories affirm who we are. We all want affirmations that our lives have meaning. And nothing does a greater affirmation than when we connect through stories.[4]
Andrew Stanton

2. Make me care.

Wake up my emotions.

Life can have a numbing affect. We spend so much of our lives going through a me-centric, self-absorbed routine that we lose our emotional bond to the world around us. We simply forget to do what we were designed to do: **to care.**

Did you know that reading fiction is linked to empathy?

Research indicates that fiction not only affects adults, but that the more stories a child has read to them, the more empathetic that child becomes.[5] Why? Because stories have the potential to make you feel what someone else feels.

Go back and watch the first few minutes of the animated feature *Up*. Pixar makes us care intensely about a crabby, 80-year-old protagonist by creating a brilliant, nearly wordless, eight-minute short film of his love story with his wife.

This principle is what Pixar refers to as the *"golden rule"* of storytelling. Director Andrew Stanton says:

Please, emotionally, intellectually, aesthetically, just make me care. We all know what it's like to not care. You've gone through hundreds of TV channels, just switching channel after channel, and then suddenly you actually stop on one. It's already halfway over, but something's caught you and you're drawn in and you care. That's not by chance, that's by design.[6]

3. Make me hope.

Prove I can win.

I remember hearing a speaker once begin by saying,
"Life is hard and then you die."
It probably wasn't the most optimistic introduction, but it's true.

Life is hard.
It's harder for some than for others. There is only one guarantee in everyone's story:

THERE WILL BE CONFLICT.

MAKE ME SEE.
MAKE ME CARE.
MAKE ME HOPE.

That's why everybody knows Harry.
You latch on to someone who is
fighting against the odds.
You identify with their struggle to
push through.

Harry won.

Yeah, I know he was a
fictional character.
But his creator, J.K. Rowling, is real.
It was in her darkest hour that she
outlined Harry's story.

An exceptionally short-lived
marriage had imploded," she says,
"and I was jobless, a lone parent,
and as poor as it is possible to be
in modern Britain, without being
homeless. ... I was the biggest
failure I knew. I was set free,
because my greatest fear had been
realized and I was still alive, and I
still had a daughter whom I adored,
and I had an old typewriter and
a big idea. And so rock bottom
became the solid foundation on
which I rebuilt my life.[7]

Maybe that's why Harry gives hope
to so many.

**You can't really grasp the
principles of story until you
understand the potential of one
essential concept:**

IMAGINATION

Imagination is the key to the power
of story. Good stories master the
art of stimulating the imagination. I
personally think God designed your
imagination to make it possible for
you to see, care and hope.

Without imagination,
you can't see past what
you already know.

Without imagination,
you can't care how
someone else feels.

Without imagination,
you can't hope beyond your
present situation.

If you happen to be a fan of Harry, you might be interested in what J.K. Rowling says:

Imagination is not only the uniquely human capacity to envision that which is not. ... In its arguably most transformative and revelatory capacity, it is the power that enables us to empathize with humans whose experiences we have never shared.

Unlike any other creature on this planet, humans can learn and understand, without having experienced. *They can think themselves into other people's places.*[8]

By the way, imagination is one of the reasons I believe in the existence of God. Imagination suggests there is still a remnant of God's *image* present in humans that distinguishes us, as Rowling said, from every other species. Just because we are broken and dysfunctional doesn't mean there is not a reflection of God's image that gives us an intrinsic ability to
think
reason
feel
dream
imagine

It's not simply the story that is powerful; it's the way it connects with our imaginations. And in order for that to happen, there has to be a good storyteller. Why is it that some speakers move you and others don't? Why is it some authors write words that stir you and others don't? **It's how they tell the story.**

This also means that just because a story is true doesn't mean that it connects.

DON'T MISS THIS:

A STORY CAN BE FICTIONAL OR TRUE, BUT HOW EFFECTIVE IT IS DEPENDS ON HOW WELL IT ENGAGES THE IMAGINATION.

Maybe this is why Jesus was such a master of spinning parables to teach people about the character of God and show them how they should respond.

Can you imagine the Creator of the cerebrum, the one who fashioned your imagination to connect with story, crafting a story to actually tell you?

True, He had an advantage over the average storyteller.
I wonder if that's why His words were so ...
timeless
powerful
life-changing.

IT'S NOT SIMPLY THE STORY THAT IS POWERFUL; IT'S THE WAY IT CONNECTS WITH OUR IMAGINATIONS.

JESUS SAID,

Let me tell you a story so you can
get a glimpse of God's character ...
He's like a father with a rebellious son
And a rich man who goes on
a journey
And a bridegroom throwing an
incredible wedding party.

**THEN JESUS PUT US IN
THOSE STORIES, TOO. HE SAID
WE ARE—**

* The casual hiker who stumbles
  across an incredible pearl in the
  middle of a field
* The woman who badgers and
  pleads with an unjust judge
  until he gives in
* The builder furrowing his brow
  as he decides between two
  plots of land

Did you ever consider that none of
Jesus' stories were actually "true"?
In some cases, a fictional story can
move people more effectively than
a true story—if it's crafted and told
in the right way. Before we blame it
on the person who is listening, let's
be honest. Some people tell stories
better than others.

Haven't you heard the same Bible
story from different communicators?
One makes it come alive.
One kills it.
(And I don't mean "kills it" in a
positive way.)

What's the difference?
Was it the text?
Maybe one used the King James
Version, while the other used a more
"liberal" translation?

Or maybe
Some speakers simply
communicate better, because they
are more gifted—or they try harder.

Yes, I believe you should pray.
Yes, I believe you should depend on God.
But none of that should be an excuse to be careless or unprepared in presenting your message.

The church should be more passionate about helping a generation
see, care and hope
than anyone else on the planet.

If imagination holds the key to connecting with the story, shouldn't we start acting like our words matter?

Too many Christians tell the Gospel story like it ended when Jesus died and rose again.
The way I understand it, the story did not end when Jesus died.
And the mystery didn't stop when He was buried.
I'm glad when Jesus said, "It is finished" on the cross,

it didn't mean the story was over.
Even the resurrection was not God's final act.
It was actually the climactic turning point of a never-ending epic.

I happen to believe there is a lot of mystery left in this drama that God originated.
WHY?
Because I have read the book of Revelation and I'm baffled.
(I'm not sure I can trust anyone who says they fully understand that book.)
There's still a lot of mystery left in the adventure of our faith.

And you do know it takes imagination to have faith.
I think this is why, when C.S. Lewis struggled to embrace the Gospel, Tolkien described it as an "imaginative failure." He said that Lewis should understand the story of Christ was like every other good story, except "it really happened."[9] ↓

I'm not sure imagination ever stops.
If you don't believe there is more mystery left in this story,
then I'm not sure you believe in a very big God.

A God who is creative   A God who is mysterious   A God who is infinite

A God who imagined your imagination and then fashioned the idea of story to stimulate it.

Sometimes I worry that many Christians have taken the magic out of the Gospel story, what C.S. Lewis came to understand as the "deeper magic" of God's plan and purpose. The kingdom of God has a mystical component—a magical side.

There is the mystery of what actually happened during His death.

 Three days later He miraculously came back to life.

 Not long after that He magically ascended into the sky.

 Then He supernaturally possessed people with His Spirit.

This story is packed with twists and turns that ignite our imaginations. As leaders, we are called to unveil this story in such a way that we invite a generation into the wonder, discovery and passion of its essence.

Don't make the mistake of too quickly placing the story in your personal doctrinal box and trying to explain everything about an un-explainable and infinite God.

AS LEADERS, WE ARE CALLED TO UNVEIL THIS STORY IN SUCH A WAY THAT WE INVITE A GENERATION INTO THE WONDER, DISCOVERY AND PASSION OF ITS ESSENCE.

IF YOU PRETEND YOU CAN EXPLAIN EVERYTHING ABOUT GOD, YOU
WILL RAISE A GENERATION TO EMBRACE A GOD WHO IS NO BIGGER
THAN YOUR DEFINITION. THAT GOD WILL ULTIMATELY NOT BE BIG
ENOUGH TO CARRY THEM THROUGH A LIFE WHERE THEY NEED TO SEE,
CARE AND HOPE.

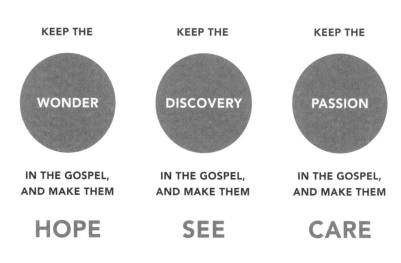

KEEP THE   **KEEP THE**   **KEEP THE**

WONDER   **DISCOVERY**   **PASSION**

IN THE GOSPEL,   **IN THE GOSPEL,**   **IN THE GOSPEL,**
AND MAKE THEM   **AND MAKE THEM**   **AND MAKE THEM**

HOPE SEE CARE

I have friends who genuinely wrestle
with their faith.
(I never do, of course.)
But one recently asked me
"I know all the Bible stories.
What else do you have for me?"

The conversation continued like this.
"So, what do you think about
the Bible?"
"I just don't get what the big deal is;
it's just a book, right?"

"Not really. It's actually a library
of 66 books. And it's written by 40
different authors over 1,600 years.
They were all very different people
ranging from nomads to kings,
from priests to fisherman. And yet
it all connects and tells one story,
about God and His love for us
through time."

"Really. I'm not sure I realized it was
all part of one story."

No one had ever connected the dots. No one had ever stirred the imagination.

It's possible to grow up reading the Bible but never understanding the story

HERE'S THE POINT.

THE ANSWER IS NOT SIMPLY TELLING THE GOSPEL STORY

IT'S HOW YOU TELL THE GOSPEL STORY.

THE ANSWER IS NOT TELLING HUNDREDS OF STORIES CHRONOLOGICALLY;

IT'S HOW YOU CONNECT WHAT YOU TEACH TO A BIGGER STORY.

THE ANSWER IS NOT JUST TELLING THE STORY OF GOD;

IT'S ALSO SHOWING THE CHARACTER OF GOD.

IT'S POSSIBLE TO GROW UP READING THE BIBLE BUT NEVER UNDERSTANDING THE STORY.

When J.K. Rowling wrote the last book about Harry, something strange happened. People were sad. It was as if a generation mourned the happy ending of a favorite story. They began to write letters and ask Rowling how Harry was doing, as if he were more than just a fictional character. People were sad because they missed Harry.

How did that happen?

Because people didn't just fall in love with the story of Harry Potter, they fell in love with Harry.

If you think the Gospel is only about the story, you're wrong.
If you think the creation of a biblical canon was the end, you're mistaken.

The power of story exists as background to invite a generation into a relationship with a ...

GOD WHO MADE THEM
GOD WHO LOVED THEM
GOD WHO REDEEMED THEM

When you try to capture the imaginations of this generation, be careful. You are not trying to get them to fall in love with a story that's already finished, but to fall in love with the Christ who rescued and redeemed them and is still alive today.

**That's why we love to say ...
It's through the story of God that you can see the character of God, and it's through seeing the character of God you can understand the story of God.**

WE ARE NOT SIMPLY TRYING TO GET A GENERATION TO LOVE THE STORY OF GOD, BUT TO FALL IN LOVE WITH THE GOD OF THE STORY.

IT'S YOUR TURN: **COLLABORATE**

ASK THESE THREE QUESTIONS TO EVALUATE YOUR
ENVIRONMENTS OR PRESENTATIONS.
HOW DO YOU MAKE PEOPLE SEE?
HOW DO YOU MAKE PEOPLE CARE?
HOW DO YOU MAKE PEOPLE HOPE?

HERE ARE SOME IDEAS
ADD YOUR OWN

PERSONALIZE IT
FOR YOU

STRATEGIZE IT
WITH YOUR TEAM

ORANGIFY IT
FOR THE NEXT GENERATION

Establish a reading list including works of fiction to help you understand the art of story-telling.

Choose a book to read together as a team that focuses on communication or the art of story-telling. Discuss ways the principles apply to your different environments.

Consider using the One Big Story series to give children or students context for the narrative of Scripture. See recommended resources.

TELL STORIES IN A WAY THAT CAPTIVATE THE HEART

CONCLUSION

I LOVE THE CHURCH

HERE ARE A FEW MORE STATS FOR YOU.

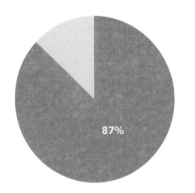

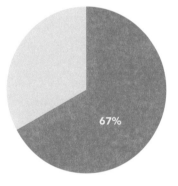

ALMOST **87 PERCENT** OF THE SUNDAYS IN MY LIFE HAVE BEEN SPENT IN CHURCH.

67 PERCENT OF THOSE WEEKENDS AS A PASTOR.

Somewhere around my eighth birthday, I became a Christian. That same year, I specifically remember telling my parents God wanted me to be a preacher. Then after I realized preachers had to speak in front of people, I changed my mind.

The closest I ever came to hearing God's voice audibly was when I was 16. The reason I think I heard God is because I actually talked back and said out loud,
"Are you sure? This doesn't make any sense."

It was the first time I remember arguing with God about something.

There's a term preachers used years ago to describe what happened to me that evening. It was called "surrendering to the ministry." Whenever I stand in front of a group of people and speak, I still think about that night ...

- hiding in an upstairs church bathroom
- crying in front of the mirror
- telling God He was making a mistake.
- surrendering.

Since that day 36 years ago, I have been a student pastor, college pastor, marrieds pastor, singles pastor, teaching pastor, and family pastor.

I have never felt qualified, talented, or experienced enough to do what I do.
It's just what I thought God told me to do.

BUT PLEASE BELIEVE ME WHEN I SAY:

I LOVE THE CHURCH.
I BELIEVE IN ITS MISSION.
I HAVE GIVEN MY LIFE TO THIS ADVENTURE.

Just in case you were wondering, I don't really believe in zombies, I rarely watch football, But I do have faith in the power of the Gospel.

I MEMORIZED THIS VERSE WHEN I WAS 16.
IF I HAD A THEME VERSE FOR MY LIFE, IT WOULD BE GALATIANS 2:20:

I HAVE BEEN CRUCIFIED WITH CHRIST AND I NO LONGER LIVE, BUT CHRIST LIVES IN ME. THE LIFE I NOW LIVE IN THE BODY, I LIVE BY FAITH IN THE SON OF GOD, WHO LOVED ME AND GAVE HIMSELF FOR ME.

Those of you who invest your life in the work of the local church have one of the most important jobs on the planet. That's why you can't be satisfied with a style or model of church that becomes irrelevant or ineffective.

Deciding what to do next can seem overwhelming. So much is changing around us. As you consider the 10 game-changers in this book, I hope you will develop a "holy" dissatisfaction for the way things are. Maybe these chapters will stimulate many conversations and be a catalyst for significant changes in your game plan. But while you are trying to decide what is next for your team or ministry, I'd like to ask you to consider doing just one thing:

MAKE A FRIEND WITH SOMEONE WHO DOESN'T GO TO CHURCH OR BELIEVE WHAT YOU DO.

When you spend time with people
who hurt,
who don't believe,
who need a faith community,
they have a way of keeping you focused.

They will help you make this personal.
They will inspire you to make critical changes.

INVITE SOMEONE INTO YOUR LIFE WHO WILL REMIND YOU THAT ...

THERE'S TOO MUCH AT STAKE FOR THE AVERAGE CHURCH TO KEEP DOING BUSINESS AS USUAL.

HERE'S A REVIEW:

THERE IS A GROWING FRUSTRATION WITH ANY CHURCHES WHO DO NOT PASSIONATELY RESPOND TO A BROKEN WORLD.

PEOPLE ARE EMBRACING DIVERSITY AND REJECTING THOSE WHO SHOW SIGNS OF INTOLERANCE.

COMMUNITIES HAVE SHIFTED AWAY FROM A SUNDAYS-ARE-FOR-CHURCH MINDSET.

THE MAJORITY OF HOMES REPRESENT FAMILIES WHO ARE STRUGGLING TO CONNECT WITHIN THE CHRISTIAN COMMUNITY.

LEADERS ARE BEING CALLED TO MODEL AUTHENTICITY AND EMPATHY.

THE ART OF COLLABORATION IS REPLACING CONVENTIONAL MODELS OF MANAGEMENT.

A NEW ECONOMIC REALITY IS CREATING AN OPPORTUNITY TO INNOVATE HEALTHIER FINANCIAL STRATEGIES.

THE RAPID GROWTH OF SOCIAL MEDIA IS INCREASING THE NEED TO CONNECT VIRTUALLY.

THE RAPID GROWTH OF SOCIAL MEDIA IS ELEVATING THE VALUE OF BEING PHYSICALLY PRESENT.

THE POWER OF STORY IS BEING REDISCOVERED IN A CULTURE THAT IS OVER-SATURATED WITH INFORMATION.

NOTES

YOUR NOTES HERE.

YOUR NOTES HERE.

YOUR NOTES HERE.

YOUR NOTES HERE.

YOUR NOTES HERE.

YOUR NOTES HERE.

MORE RESOURCES
WORKS CITED
CONTRIBUTING
VOICES